Essential
Greek
Islands

by
ARTHUR EPERON

Arthur Eperon has been a feature writer, foreign
correspondent, travel and news reporter for over 40
years. Specialising in food, wine and tourism, he has
written several travel books and contributed to a
number of magazines and newspapers. During his
career he has worked with the *Wish You Were Here*
programme and for the *New York Times*.

Produced by AA Publishing

**Written by Arthur Eperon
Peace and Quiet section
by Paul Sterry**

Edited, designed and produced
by AA Publishing. Maps ©
The Automobile Association 1994

Distributed in the United Kingdom
by AA Publishing, Fanum House,
Basingstoke, Hampshire, RG21 2EA.

First published 1990
Revised Second edition 1993
Revised Third edition © The
Automobile Association 1994.

A CIP catalogue record for this book is
available from the British Library.

ISBN 0 7495 0838 8

Published by AA Publishing, which is a
trading name of Automobile
Association Developments Limited,
whose registered office is Fanum
House, Basingstoke, Hampshire,
RG21 2EA.
Registered number 1878835

Colour separation: L.C. Repro,
Basingstoke

Printed by: Printers Trento, S.R.L., Italy

Cover picture: Thira

The islands of **Crete**, **Corfu** and
Rhodes (shown in light orange
on the maps) are not described
in this guide, but are covered by
separate titles in the *Essential*
Series. (See inside front cover
for a full list of *Essential* titles.)

English spellings of place-names

The visitor to Greece will find
there are several alternatives. In
general, this book uses the more
common spellings. An
alternative (corresponding with
the maps) is given in brackets in
the text headings and in the
index.
However, while a few may be
confusing, most place-names
involve a difference of only a
letter or two, eg Skyros and
Skiros, and can easily be
identified.

CONTENTS

MAPS AND PLANS

This book employs a simple
rating system to help choose
which places to visit:

 'top ten'

◆◆◆ do not miss
◆◆   see if you can
◆   worth seeing if you
     have time

Country Distinguishing Signs
On several maps, international
distinguishing signs have been
used to indicate the location of
the countries which surround the
Greek Islands. Thus:

Ⓖ = Greece
Ⓣ = Turkey

INTRODUCTION

You go to the smaller Greek islands to relax and rejuvenate. You go for sun, for lazing, to enjoy the beauty of the countryside and the sea. If you want organisation and order on holiday, or if you like to plan your sightseeing and evening action to a timetable, you will be very frustrated.

On the big tourist islands of Corfu, Rhodes and Crete (described in other *Essential* guides), you can find international hotels with smooth service and such comforts as efficient lifts and modern bathrooms. Even the buses may run on time. On small islands such trappings do not matter, and after a few hours you will not care, either.

You will learn again to take delight in simpler things, like the silver light on the blue sea, sun on white houses with blue doors and shutters, conversation, friendship and the smell of dishes cooking in copper pans on the stove of a taverna. You will delight in the wildflowers which decorate the fields and ditches of farms which know no weedkillers: poppies and many-coloured buttercups, purple Venus's looking-glass, yellow and white crown daisies and dozens more flourish prolifically in spring,

Despite the growing number of visitors, Skopelos remains a quiet and undeveloped island, perfect for a get-away-from-it-all holiday

while wild crocuses and little sweet-scented narcissi bloom in autumn.

You may find yourself passing an hour watching a fishing boat sail over the horizon or a donkey trudging up a hillside, and you will not regard it as time wasted.

Eccentric plumbing turns some people against the Greek Islands. The water may go off for hours during the summer when water becomes precious. The floor of the shower room in your pension may flood to 3 inches before the primitive drain copes. But it will soon dry and so will your feet. Clothes are no problem. You need only be semi-formal if you enter a church or monastery and you will have little chance to show off your holiday wardrobe. Your jeans or slacks will dry in the sun between breakfast and supper; meantime you can live in your bathing costume and a shirt.

Of course, tourism has changed the Greek Isles, bringing some prosperity and a more bearable life, so that young men no longer have to emigrate to Athens, the US or Australia to escape the primitive poverty. Improved communications have done most to change the Isles. It may have been romantic for tourists and wanderers to travel between islands balanced astride a cask of wine between a goat and a guitar-player, drinking from a communal wine bottle, but it was not much fun for Greek grandmas and grandpas visiting their children, nor for men on inter-island business trips. The smaller Greek Isles are *not* 'spoiled'. A few Isles get crowded in mid-summer, but only in certain tourist areas. Brave the lanes and old mule tracks which pass as roads in the interior or remoter coasts, and you will find deserted coves and lonely rocks and villages where goats and vines are of far more pressing interest than passing tourists. Anyway, mid-summer can be too hot and local people too busy. Some Isles, such as the Cyclades, can be windy in April when the weather and ferries are unpredictable. May is more settled and beautiful. June starts to get hot. September is delightful in most isles and October balmy and pleasant in the more southerly ones, with few other tourists about. But there is no 'best time' to go to the Greek Isles. It is a personal matter.

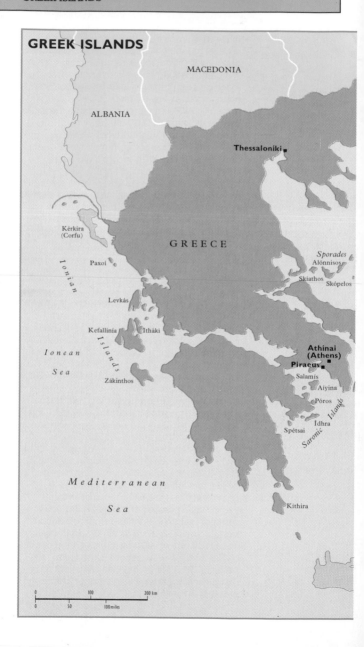

GREEK ISLANDS

MACEDONIA

ALBANIA

Thessaloniki

Kérkira
(Corfu)

GREECE

Sporades
Alónnisos

Paxoí

Skiathos

Skópelos

Ionian

Levkás

Islands

Kefallinía

Itháki

**Athínai
(Athens)**
Piraeus

Ionean

Sea

Salamís

Zákinthos

Aíyina

Póros

Saronic Islands

Spétsai

Ídhra

Mediterranean

Sea

Kithira

| 0 | 100 | 200 km |

| 0 | 50 | 100 miles |

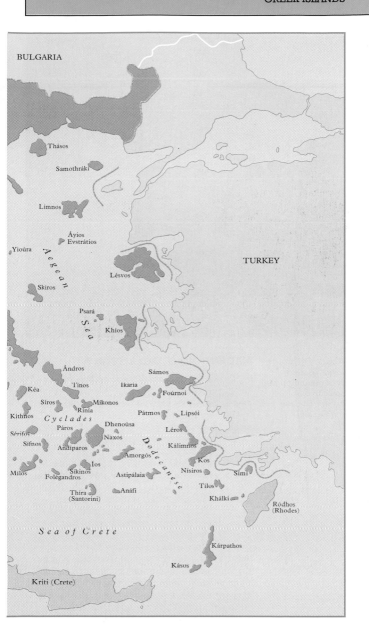

Woods and groves cover Skiathos, even growing right down to the sweeps of clean yellow sand

BACKGROUND AND HISTORY

All Greek Islands are different in history and scenery. Some are lush and green, others have near-lunar landscapes of volcanic rock with a sprinkling of shrubs and trees. At times neighbouring isles were sworn enemies, and you can still hear old men call people of the next island 'pirates' or 'robbers'.

Classical Greece was by no means a united country. It was a series of city-states when the Persians set out to conquer it in the 5th century BC. Some islands sided with the Persians against Athens – a choice they rued after the unexpected victories of the Greeks over the mighty Persian Empire at Marathon and Salamis (480BC). More isles backed the Spartans against Athens in the fearsome Peloponnesian War from 431 to 404BC. Various isles were taken over by various rulers, from the Venetians to the Byzantine Empire and the Knights of St John of Jerusalem, with Christian warriors fighting the Muslems, especially the Turks.

The Turks ruled most of Greece from the 15th century until 1829, usually with harshness and corruption. They forbade schooling in the Greek language, so education was kept alive secretly by monks in monasteries. The conquerors levelled crippling taxes to pay for the Turkish army and navy and took away quotas of pretty girls each year for their harems, so that Greek mothers prayed that their daughters would be ugly. And they took the eldest sons from every family to be Janissaries; they were brought up as Muslims and trained to be soldiers and sailors fighting for Turkey. But some islands did not fall to the Turks for some time. Crete resisted until 1669, little Tinos until 1718. Some islands prospered under the Turks. Symi had enormous privileges because it built the fast-sailing *skaphes* which the Turks used for courier boats. Chios was given special privileges for producing mastika, which two ladies of the Turkish Sultan's harem loved to chew (later it was used for chewing-gum). The Turks admired the Greek Island sailors and crewed ships with them, so the islanders kept their sailing tradition. But some islands, left unguarded by the Turks, were raided by pirates such as the fearsome

Santorini is covered with pumice and lava, legacy of countless volcanic eruptions over the centuries; it is not, therefore, a particularly attractive island, but it is most spectacular

BACKGROUND/HISTORY

This elderly couple from Skopelos are typical of the friendly people of the Greek Isles

Barbarossa, who plundered and destroyed them and took their people to sell as slaves. So the islanders ran the Turkish blockade as smugglers and turned to piracy themselves. It was these island sailors, especially from the Saronic isles of Hydra, Spetses and Aegina, who in 1821 started the War of Independence. They enjoyed several splendid victories, and the guerilla leaders (Klepht) set up their headquarters on Skopelos and Skiathos. The Turks were finally beaten in 1827 by an Allied fleet from Britain, France and Russia, which, under Admiral Codrington, annihilated the Turkish fleet at Navarino, and most of Greece was freed. But piracy had become a habit with the islanders. Admiral Codrington had to inform them that unless they stopped it, the Royal Navy would sink *their* ships as he had sunk the Turks! Inexplicably, the Allies gave the 12 Dodecanese Islands, including Rhodes, back to Turkey. Then the Italians took them in 1912 and Mussolini tried to 'Italianise' them. They did not join Greece until 1947.

With so many occupiers seeking to suppress Greek culture over so many centuries, and with such varying histories, it is surprising that the island people have kept their essential Greekness and loyalty to Greece, and that they do not vary even more than they do now.

One thing the islands have in common to this day, together with their love of the sea, which still rules their lives, is a distrust and awe of Athens, which seems to them to rule and tax them like an absentee landlord.

WHAT TO SEE

SARONIC ISLES

AEGINA (AIYINA)

Only 40 minutes by hydrofoil, or
1½ hours by ferry, from Piraeus,
Aegina remains an independent
island quite different from Athens.
The atmosphere is carefree and
happy. Weekend invasions by
Athenians, its growing popularity
with foreign visitors and cruise
passengers making a quick trip
to the magnificent temple of
Aphaia, have changed it, but
not fundamentally. Fishing and
agriculture are still more
important than tourism, though
fish scarcities are beginning to
hurt. Growing pistachio nuts is
particularly lucrative. They are
harvested in August. Aegina is
pronounced 'Ayina', with the
stress on the first A.

◆◆
AEGINA (AIYINA) TOWN

It is proud to have been, in
1826, the first capital of Free
Greece during the fight for
independence against the Turks.
The first president, Capodistria,
set up the Greek government
here. The first free newspaper
was published, the first drachma
minted carrying a phoenix head
to show Greece risen from the
ashes. The austere pink tower of
Markellos was the first building
of Free Greece. What is now the
pubic library was the Residence
of the President, who worked
and slept upstairs while drachma
were minted below. Capodistria
moved to Nauplion in the
Peloponnese in 1829 because
the Allied fleet was there. He was
murdered by Greek political
opponents. Aegina now has a
busy main harbour (a present
from an American, Samuel
Greenly Howe) and a fishing
harbour lined with coloured
boats and a tiny quayside
fisherman's chapel of Aghios
Nikolaos, patron saint of sailors.
Fishermen catch a lot of *marides*
(whitebait). You can step across
the gangplanks of boats to buy
your vegetables, fruit and fish,
laid out as if in a shop. There are
few tourist, souvenir or clothes
shops for foreigners. Shops, bars
and restaurants are mostly
aimed at locals or Athenians.
Only one column survives of
Apollo's Temple on Kolona hill,
but there is an archaeological
museum (open 08.30–15.00hrs
Tuesday–Saturday; 10.00–15.00hrs
Sunday; closed Monday). A
walk northwards takes you to
Livadi, where a plaque marks
the whitewashed house where
the Cretan Nikos Kazantzakis
wrote *Zorba the Greek*.

*The 5th-century BC Temple of Aphaia
on Aegina is one of the most beautiful
Classical temples in Greece*

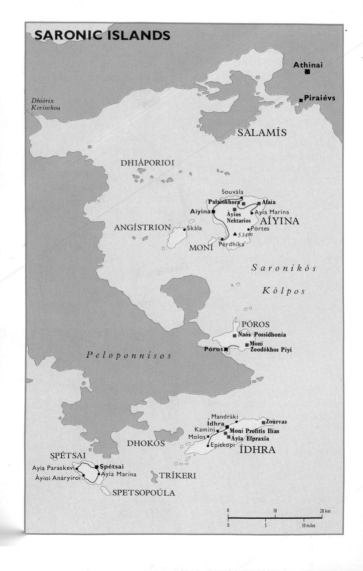

*The colourful fishing harbour in
Aegina Town*

◆◆◆
PERDIKA (PERDHIKA)
Five and a half miles (9km)
south from Aegina Town,
Perdika is a charming fishing
village with a line of good fish
restaurants where you choose
your fish then drink your wine
on the white terrace above the
fishing boats while the fish are
grilled over charcoal.

◆◆
MONI
From Perdika you can see the
delightful little isle of Moni,
seemingly a stone's throw
away. Named because it used
to belong to a monastery, it now
belongs to the Touring Club of
Greece and you pay a small
entrance fee on your boat fare.
There is a campsite in summer,
beautifully clear water, a small
beach, footpaths through
woods, then rocky scrub
pungent with wild herbs,

especially sage (which is made
into tea as a blood purifier).
Wild flowers bloom from spring
until September. Peacocks may
join you on the beach, and
hiding in the shrub are splendid
but shy wild kri-kri goats with
great long horns. Boats from
Perdika take 10 minutes to Moni.

◆
HELLANION
Inland towards Portes is
Hellanion, 11 miles (18km) from
Aegina Town, where Aikos, son
of Aegina, prayed to Zeus for
rain during a drought all over
Greece. Zeus granted his
request – not surprisingly, for
Zeus was his father. (Aegina was
one of the hundreds of
mistresses of the aptly-named
Father of the Gods.)

◆
SOUVALA
A delightful little port and spa for
treating rheumatism and skin
diseases. Here you can get away
from the intense summer heat.

Ferries call direct from Piraeus. You can eat and drink in the evening at harbourside tavernas while you watch the fishing boats go out. Souvala is northeast of Aegina Town, and the road to it passes Kipseli, where there are views to the port from the taverna. Kipseli means 'beehive'. The village was called Halasmeni (ruined) until recently, after the ruins of a church. But local girls complained!

◆◆
AGHIA (AYIA) MARINA

Aghia Marina, on the east coast, 8½ miles (14km) from Aegina Town is the tourist resort of Aegina, built up recently and a little too fast from a seaside village. It is a superb place for children, for sands stretch a long way round the almost landlocked bay and the water is shallow and safe. There are pedalos for hire. Tavernas and restaurants with tables under umbrellas line the sands. There are pensions, small self-catering blocks and small hotels, including the comfortable Apollo in a fine position on high rocks. Even its swimming pool has a fine view. Small boats bring cruise passengers ashore. They are herded into coaches and taken up the hill to see the Temple of Aphaia, then they shop for souvenirs in Aghia Marina and are gone within 2 hours.

Four miles (6.5km) along and just south of the road from Aegina to Aghia Marina is the monastery of Aghios (Ayios) Nektarios, named after a bishop of Aegina who was canonised in 1961, the most recent Greek Orthodox Church saint. The original chapel is reserved for women. The saint's remains are in a new chapel. Twenty-two nuns live in the monastery. Opposite the monastery set on a low hill are the ruins of the former Byzantine and medieval capital Palaiochora (Palaiokhora), founded in the 9th century AD after a very bloody Arab pirate attack on Aegina Town. But in 1537 the pirate-admiral Barbarossa took Palaiochora, massacred the men and took away 6,000 women and children as slaves. With Independence in 1826, the people moved back to the coast, dismantling much of their hill capital to build the new one. There were originally 365 13th-century churches in Palaiochora, only 28 have survived.

◆◆◆
TEMPLE OF APHAIA (AFAÍA)

The temple, built in beautiful Doric style, stands in a superb position on a wooded ridge with sea views on two sides. One of the most beautiful and complete classical temples in Greece, it was built between 480 and 410BC and its lovely columns narrowing from the base to the capital are much like those of the Parthenon. Twenty-five of the original 32 columns are still there. Alas, the splendid pediment statues were sold in 1811, by the German and British archaeologists who dug them up, to the eccentric King Ludwig of Bavaria. They are now in the Glyptothek Museum in Munich. The temple was dedicated to Aphaia, a goddess little known outside Aegina. She was either a moon goddess or a Minoan goddess of wisdom and light from Crete. The temple is 9 miles (14km) east of Aegina Town, on a hill above Aghia Marina. Don't miss it.

Accommodation

There are plenty of hotels especially at Aghia Marina. Most of those in Aegina Town are old. **The Hotel Brown**, 3 Toti Hatzi, is friendly, C-class (tel: (0297) 22271); the **Danae** is B-class (tel: (0297) 22424). The **Apollo** with a swimming pool and nice terrace views, is the best in Aghia Marina (tel: (0297) 32271/4).

Restaurants (Aegina)

The restaurants and tavernas on the island serve above-average meals. Fish can be outstanding, especially at Perdika. **Costas**, just outside Aghia Marina serves good Greek dishes.

General information

Population 11,500
Area 32 sq miles (83 sq km)
17 nautical miles from Piraeus.
Tourist Office & Tourist Police: (tel: (0297) 22391/23333).
Harbour Police: (tel: (0297) 22328).

How to get there

Ferries: there are about 10 daily from Piraeus, mostly going to Aegina Town, but some call at Aghia Marina and Souvala in summer (1½ hrs).
Hydrofoil: from Piraeus, every hour in summer (40 mins); fewer in winter. Summer cruise ships make the round trip from Piraeus to Aegina, Poros, Hydra, Spetses and back. Boat trips can be made from the island to Hydra and Poros.

POROS

Poros consists of two islands connected by a bridge. Its capital, Poros Town, on the smaller island, is so close to Galatos on the Peloponnese mainland that Henry Miller in *The Colossus of Maroussi* compared his arrival to sailing through the streets of Venice. The strait is only 280 yds (256m) wide. Sea taxis called *benzina* pop across constantly.

◆◆
POROS TOWN

As you approach, you see two uneven humps with dark green lemon groves; then, as you sail through a narrow, almost secretive entrance into an open bay, the houses of Poros Town

Churches – these are church roof tiles – and houses jostle together busily in Poros Town

appear, like white cubes piled up the sides of a cone. The town has a happy atmosphere. One reason is that the harbour-quay is a market, with stalls selling vegetables, fruit and fish as well as souvenirs and clothes. The stalls share the space with the tables and chairs of bars.
The hump (called Sferia) on which Poros port is sited is small enough to walk round in an hour. A causeway leads to the bigger hump (Kalavaria) which is greener, with several coves of shingle shaded by pine. It has a short stretch of tarmac road leading in 2 miles (3km) to Askeli bay in the south, where most of the tourist hotels are. Overlooking the bay is the attractive 18th-century Zoodochos Pughi (Moní Zoodokhos Piyi) monastery.

◆
TEMPLE OF POSEIDON (Naós Possidhonía)
Only a few stone walls remain of the great temple of Poseidon, 9 miles (14km) north of Poros Town, built in 500BC and once as magnificent as the Aegina temple. In the 18th century its marble blocks were looted, cut into sizes mules could carry, taken to the shore and shipped to Hydra to build a monastery. The temple was a sanctuary: any fugitive or shipwreck victim was safe within its walls.
Poros makes its living from fishing, tourism and especially growing lemons, olives and flowers. Visitors wonder where they grow all these crops until they discover that many farmers also have land across the Galatas straits on the mainland, 5 minutes

by boat. Here is Lemonodassos (the Lemon Forest), with 30,000 lemon trees.

Accommodation
There are two recommended hotels in Poros Town: the **Hotel Poros** has wonderful sweeping views, B-class (tel: (0298) 22216/8); the **Anessis** (tel: (0298) 22111) is a pleasant, though fairly expensive, pension.

Restaurants
The **Lagoudera** restaurant on Poros waterfront is one of the best on these islands, serving superb (if pricey) fish.

General information
Population 4,000
Area 9 sq miles (23 sq km)
31 nautical miles from Piraeus.
Tourist Office & Tourist Police: (tel: (0298) 22256 or 22462).
Harbour Police: (tel: (0298) 22274).

How to get there
Ferries: the car ferry from Piraeus, Aegina and Methana (on the mainland) calls at Poros three times a day (3¾ hours); it continues to Hydra. There are regular ferries from the island to Galata on the mainland.
Hydrofoil: every 1 or 2 hours from Zea Marina, Piraeus (1hr).

HYDRA (IDHRA)
Though most visitors stay on Hydra only a few hours, it has devoted fans and has been called 'the Greek St Tropez'. At first sight this is surprising, for it is bare and rocky, with no good beaches and is often short of water. Cars are banned. You must walk or cycle in the hot sun to see anything outside the port. It is desperately short of

Bird's-eye view of the harbour at Hydra, one of the loveliest of the Isles

accommodation because local laws forbid the building of those square concrete boxes which spoil some Greek villages, and, without a reservation, you will not find a room in mid-summer. Old cottages and farms have been repaired for holiday homes. The heavy stone Venetian-style mansions with beautiful Italianate interiors, have been restored strictly to their original style. The port is particularly photogenic and cosmopolitan. In mid-summer Hydra is crowded and very hot at mid-day. May and September are delightful. Most of the splendid old villas are private houses. They were built by shipowners, for Hydriots were skilled sailors. A few houses can be visited. Genuine professional artists are especially welcome at the old house of the Tombazis family, now a School of Fine Art. The Tsamados house is now a Merchant Marine School. This has a bar open to the public (To Laikon). Ask at the door if you can see round both of these One or two owners open their villas at times on application. Ask at the Town Hall.

A long walk of about 1½ hrs by lanes and paths leads to the Twin Monastery of Profitis Elias (Moní Profitis Ilías) and Convent of Aghia Efpraxia (Áyia

Bare and rocky, Hydra is still a working fishing island

Efpraxia). The monastery was founded by refugees from Mount Athos in 1770 and no woman may enter. A few nuns still weave but embroider at the convent and you can buy their work (mostly shawls). You can hire a mule to get here but it is pricey and uncomfortable. There are lovely views.

◆
KAMINI
Just over a mile (2km) south of the port is Kamini, with a small harbour, tavernas and shops. You can swim off the rocks here. Further down this coast is Molos, where there is a cove for swimming beside a pine forest.

Accommodation
Miramare Hotel (tel: (0298) 52300/1) at Mandraki is A-class but you must book half-pension. The **Hydra** at 8 Voulgari, (tel: (0298) 52102) is in a fine sea-captain's mansion.

Restaurants
Restaurants on the portside are pricey and good fun. The **Three Brothers** restaurant near the cathedral is cheaper and offers very good Greek dishes.

General information
Population 2,750
Area 19½ sq miles (50 sq km)
38 nautical miles from Piraeus.
Tourist Office & Tourist Police: Navarchou N Botsi Street (tel: (0298) 52205 — season only).
Harbour Police: (tel: (0298) 52279).

How to get there
Ferries: There is one ferry daily from Piraeus (4hrs 10 mins). Some call at Aegina, Methana (on the mainland) and Poros. Regular boats sail to Ermoni on mainland (½hr).
Hydrofoil: 5 times a day from Piraeus (Zea Marina), calling at Aegina and Poros (1½hrs).

SPETSES (SPETSAI)
You can walk round this charming isle in a day. Two-thirds of it is covered in pines and all around the coast are little coves you must reach finally on foot or by sea. No cars are allowed but there are two taxis and one bus, and a partly-tarmac road around the isle resounds to the clomp of horses' hoofs. Horse-drawn fiacres are the main transport. You can hire bicycles, too.
Spetses has been a holiday isle

for Athenians since the grand old Possidonion Hotel was built in 1914. It is still open. With a casino operating between the World Wars, it was *the* resort of Greece until the 1960s.

◆◆◆
SPETSES TOWN
The capital and port (officially called Spetses but known locally as Dapia after the square near the harbour) spreads for 1¾ miles (3km) along the coast. The Dapia, sprinkled with old cannons, is particularly lively, with fashionable restaurants and bars brightly lit at night. The cheaper bars and tavernas are around the fish market. Old family mansions include the home of the powerful ship-owning Mexis family, now a museum. Built in 1795, the house, half Venetian, half Moorish in style, was like a fortress surrounded by high walls – not for privacy but defence against rival rich shipping families. In the museum itself, among 19th century local paintings and costumes, is the 'Freedom or Death' flag of the War of Independence, and a casket with the remains of the local Independence heroine Lascarina Bouboulina – a most bellicose admiral. A rich widow with nine children, she continued her father's businesses of making ships and of piracy against Turkish allies. In the Revolution, dressed in the striped costume of Spetses and carrying a cutlass, she led her ships in big naval engagements, often landing to lead her forces. Narrow, cobbled alleyways in the town are inlaid with mythical

marine figures made from coloured pebbles. By the old harbour (now used by yachts) and the town beach, is a memorial marking the naval battle of 8 September 1822, when Spetsiot brigs and fireships repelled a superior Turkish force. On the nearest weekend to 8 September the scene is re-enacted each year in a regatta with fireworks replacing gunfire. Beside the harbour are large white houses and the cathedral of Aghios Nikolaos, once a monastery. On its clock tower the flag of freedom was first raised in 1821.

◆
AGHII ANARGYROI (AYIOI ANARYIROI)
Of the many coves along the jagged coastline, the most developed is the shady Aghii Anargyroi, where a village has built up around holiday homes, with a good taverna. Small boats call, the bus stops in summer, or you can walk to it round the road – about 9 miles (15km) – or on island paths. High on a point between here and the little beach of Aghia Paraskevi is the large Villa Yasemia (Jasmine), known as the 'House of Magus'. To readers of John Fowles' novel *The Magus*, it is 'Bourani'. Fowles taught at the imposing Anargyrios and Korgialenios School 1¼ miles (2km) west of Spetses Town, founded in 1927 on the model of an English public school.

◆
AGHIA (AYIA) MARINA
The beach here, a mile (2km) south from the old harbour, is very popular in summer.

◆
VRELLO

The lovely valley Vrello at the northeast tip of the island, 3¾ miles (6km) from the harbour, is the beauty spot of Spetses.

Accommodation

The old **Possidonion** (tel: 0298) 72308) is A-class. **Kasteli**, also class A, has hotel rooms and bungalows (tel: (0298) 72311). **Myrtoon**, C-class, has a roof garden and bar (tel: (0298) 72555). Hotels are booked well in advance. You may well have to settle for a room in a private house. There is no campsite.

Restaurants

The cooking in restaurants is better than on most isles, and dearer. Speciality is sea bream in a very spicy sauce (*psari*

Spetsiotiko). **Mandalena's** restaurant on the new harbour waterfront serves good seafood.

General information

Population 3,750
Area 8½ sq miles (22 sq km)
53 nautical miles from Piraeus.
Tourist Office & Tourist Police: Botsari Street (tel: (0298) 73100).
Harbour Police: (tel: (0298) 72245).

How to get there

Ferries: One daily from Piraeus (almost 5½hrs). There are frequent boats to Kosta Ermioni and Porto Heli on mainland, and one goes daily to Nauplion.
Hydrofoil: regular service from Zea Marina, Piraeus (2hrs).

On the wooded isle of Spetses, trees sometimes grow down to the beach

CYCLADES

ANDROS

A big mountainous island, wooded, well watered with many olives and vines. Andros seems better-organised and more prosperous than the other Cyclades Islands, and has fairly few foreign tourists.

It is reached easily from Athens, so it has become a hideaway for well-heeled Athenians. Ironic, for Andros sided through history with the enemies of Athens, even with the Persians at Salamis. Boats leave the mainland from the scruffy port of Rafina, less than an hour by car or bus from Athens, and land you at the port of Gavrion, which is a bad advertisement for Andros. It has a big lorry park, uninviting-looking cafés and a temporary look. But a short bus journey soon shows you the island's scenic attraction and undeveloped coastline.

◆◆
BATSI

Most foreign visitors stay at the one resort which is slightly developed. Batsi, on a bus route 5 miles (8km) from Gavrion. It is the easiest place to find a bed. It is in a sheltered bay, with a fishing harbour at one end and a grass covered sand dune with a beach at the other. A beach with some trees for shade joins them, backed at the harbour end by old-style shops, including one of those very-Greek general stores serving everything from food and wine to books, brooms and nails. There are lively tavernas on the dockside with tables under vines, all specialising in fish. And there are two banks. A few small hotels round the bay bring you to three small, new two-storey apartment blocks. The village is backed by tiers of red-roofed houses reached by steps and terraced farms.

ANDROS TOWN

Buses continue from Batsi past the ancient capital of Paliopolis, of which some walls remain, to the capital and port Andros Town on the east coast. It is a working town still involved in shipping, and is pleasant and interesting. It is built mostly on a finger of land above two good sandy beaches, with remains of a Venetian castle on the end, several museums, and puzzling changes of level.

The main street with old mansions and marble paving is for pedestrians. It leads to a charming little square, Kairis, where you can admire good sea views while taking a drink or a meal, outside or in. Stenies, 3 miles (5km) from the town, has a good beach.

A right branch of the road from Batsi to Andros leads over Mount Gerakonos to the fishing port of Ormos Korthion, 18½ miles (30km) from Batsi. It has a small C-class hotel, Korthion, rooms and restaurants in lanes off the main street. On the road here you pass Palaiokastro, a nice old village with ruins of another Venetian fort.

The road north from Gavrion turns into a track which leads to mountain villages, including attractive Amolohos. A surfaced road leads to the Tower of Aghios Petros, which dates

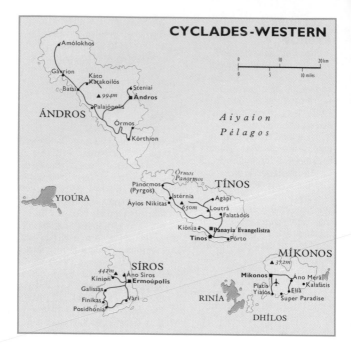

CYCLADES-WESTERN

from the Hellenistic period – 65ft (20m) high, its upper storeys are reached by a ladder. No one knows whether it was for storing food, a fort or signalling tower. Three miles (5km) above Batsi is the village of Kato Katakilos, with a stream running through it, three lively tavernas with music and exuberant dancing in season.

Accommodation
Hotel Paradissos in Andros is elegant, old-style and B-class (tel: (0282) 22187). **Aegli** up some steps off the high street is C-class (tel: (0282) 22303). Gavrion: **Gavrion Beach Hotel** is good for C-class (tel: (0282) 71312), as is **Korthion** (tel: (0282) 61218) in Korthion.

Restaurants
The best restaurants are near the beach in Andros Town and near the harbour at Batsi, where the very best is **Yiannis**' taverna, below the steps on the esplanade. Yiannis has a farm and serves good meat from it. The **Lykion** in Batsi serves good value dishes and is pleasant.

General information
Population 9,500
Area 144 sq miles (373 sq km)
89 nautical miles from Piraeus.
Tourist Office: (tel: (0282) 71250).
Tourist Police: in Gavrion police station (tel: (0282) 71220).

How to get there
Ferries: There is no direct ferry

from Piraeus. Take a bus from Athens to Rafina (55mins) then a ferry to Andros (2½hrs). Some Rafina ferries call at Tinos and Syros, others call at Tinos and Mykonos. There are daily ferries from Andros to Tinos (2hrs).

TINOS

A holy island to modern Greeks, Tinos has been called the 'Orthodox Lourdes'. Pilgrims arrive on the Feast Days of the Virgin: 25 March (The Annunciation) and 15 August (the Assumption).

◆◆

TINOS TOWN

The pilgrimage centre in Tinos Town is the neo-classical Church of Panaghia Evangelistria (Annunciation), which is hung with hundreds of votive offerings and lamps in silver and even gold, given in thanks by the faithful who still flock here to seek spiritual comfort, relief from afflictions and, perhaps, a miracle cure. During the weeks of the Feasts people queue to kiss the ikon, now decked in gold, diamonds and pearls.

In July 1822, an 80-year-old nun from a local convent, Sister Panaghia (now a saint), dreamed that the Virgin revealed to her where an ikon could be found in a field. Excavations found the treasure near a ruined church, so the new church was built there. The ikon was discovered just as the Greek fight for freedom from the Turks had begun, so it was hailed as a sign from God and the church is a national shrine. The crypt of the original ruined church, now a chapel, has a

spring believed to have curative powers. In a mausoleum alongside are the victims of the cruiser *Elli*. When the festival was at its height on 15 August 1940, an Italian submarine sneaked into Tinos harbour and sank the cruiser. The two countries were not at war. The sinking vitalised Greek resistance, and infuriated the powerful Greek lobby in the US (still not in the war).

Tinos Town is rich in museums, including a painting gallery with works of the Ionian School and a Rubens. The archaeological museum (08.30–15.00hrs; closed Mondays) includes finds from the Sanctuary of Poseidon and Amphitrite, 2½ miles (4km) northwest of the town at Kionia, which also has two beaches and a good hotel (the Tinos Beach).

In pilgrimage weeks a great many candles are lit in the revered church in Tinos Town

Less crowded beaches near the town are at Aghios Sostis, 4½ miles (7km) away, a sweeping sandy beach, and Porto, 5 miles (8km) away, with new low-built apartments, but no taverna yet. A bus goes from the town pier to the large 12th-century Kechrovounio Convent where the sister had her dream; her embalmed head is here.

◆◆
WEST COAST

The island's west coast has steep tracks to the sea, and gritty beaches. A mountainous main road leads to Ormos Pánormos (Pyrgos locally), 20½ miles/33km from Tinos Town, where artists work in green marble. There is a museum, a school of Fine Art and an attractive square with shops selling students' work. This is the green part of the island. From Isternia, a picturesque village just south, a steep paved road leads to Aghios Nikitas beach – pebbly with a shady cove. This is a big old quay, a hotel, some tavernas, rooms and tranquillity.

Accommodation

Tinion, 1 C Alavanou (tel: (0283) 22261), B-class, is one of the oldest hotels and is still pleasant and friendly.
Poseidonion, 4 Paralias (tel: (0283) 22245) along the Esplanade, over a good restaurant, is above C-class average, and most of its rooms have wc and shower. **Eleana**, Paralias (tel: (0283) 22561), beside Aghios Ioannon Church, is above average for D-class. The best hotel is the **Tinos Beach** at Aghios Kokas Beach, Kionia (tel: (0283) 22626/8).

Restaurants

Because of the festivals, Tinos Town has plenty of restaurants, tavernas and hotels, **Michalis Taverna**, Gavou Street, is one of the best places to eat.

General information

Population 7,700
Area 75 sq miles (195 sq km)
86 nautical miles from Piraeus.
Tourist Office: (tel: (0283) 23513). Tourist Police: (tel: (0283) 22255).

How to get there

Ferries: Once or twice a day from Piraeus (via Siros, 4¾hrs) and from Rafina on the mainland (via Andros, 4hrs). Also frequent services from Andros and Mykonos; less frequent from Syros. Summer ferries go to Paros and Naxos.

MYKONOS (MIKONOS) ✓

Mykonos is still the most fashionable isle in Greece, where Athenians love to own a house. It is rocky and windy, though pretty, with delicate windmills, 365 churches built as votive offerings to heaven, and a lot of beaches.
There is night life of most sorts and the isle is great fun for a few days and nights. Shops in the alleys of the old port sell overpriced jewellery, gold and furs, and, like the streets, get very crowded when cruise passengers arrive. The fashionable beaches are still Paradise, Platis Yialos and Super Paradise, which is unofficially nudist and beloved by gays. Less crowded beaches are at Elia, Anna Bay and the two coves between Paradise and

Mykonos is a fashionable place, where a lot of sitting and watching-of-the-world goes on

Yialos. The best way to reach beaches in summer is by caique from the harbour. Pick your beach according to the wind. The centre of the isle is rock and gets very hot in summer.

◆◆◆
KHORA (MIKONOS TOWN)

The Khora, the photogenic port and capital, is well whitewashed, neat and gleaming, barred to traffic and is most alluring, particularly the Alefkandra ('Little Venice') area. The Archaeological Museum has interesting unusual vases, and funeral jewellery and headstones from the 1st and 2nd centuries BC, taken from Rineia island where the old and sick from the nearby isle of Delos were sent to die.

◆◆◆
DELOS (DHILOS)

Our forefathers used Mykonos simply as a base to see the archaeological sites on Delos, the island sanctuary dedicated to Apollo and as important as Delphi to the Ancient Greeks. French archaeologists have excavated the site since 1872 and have done a good job of reconstruction of what is left. Boats leave daily from Mykonos at about 08.30–09.00hrs returning at 12.30hrs (½ hr trip).

Accommodation

Hotels and restaurants are dearer and smarter than on most other isles and food is often good. Passengers landing by ferry are almost persecuted by touts offering rooms. They will whisk away your luggage, then put you on a bus to where the room is. For those seeking action both day and night,

Windmill and cruise ship, evening light, Mykonos

Mykonos port is the place to stay, but rooms there are dearer and scarcer. The **Leto** has a wonderful harbour view, is best, most fashionable and dearest (tel: (0289) 22207). **Philippi**, 32 Kalogera Street (tel: (0289) 22295), though D-class, is charming. D-class **Platis Yialos Beach Hotel** (tel: (0289) 22913) is better and dearer than its class suggests. On Ornos Beach, 2 miles (3.5km) from Mykonos Town, is the convenient **Paralos Beach**, C-class (tel: (0289) 22600).

Restaurants
There is a big choice of tavernas and restaurants in the port and Khora. **Taverna Nikos** (behind the town hall) has a good choice, including roasts. **El Greco's**, on Odhos Enoplon Dinameon, is good, but rather pricey; it is a picturesque area at night. At Alefkandra ('Little Venice'), the **Pelican** restaurant

is beautifully placed, and serves good meals.

General information
Population 5,500 (very variable as Athenians come and go) Area 33 sq miles (85 sq km) 94 nautical miles from Piraeus. Tourist Office & Tourist Police: on quay (tel: (0289) 22482). Harbour Police: ferry end of harbour, post office building (tel: (0289) 22218).

How to get there
Air: Charters direct from Europe. Flights from Athens (50mins), 7–11 a day; Iraklion (Crete), daily (1hr 10mins); Rhodes, daily (2hrs); Santorini, daily (1hr 40mins). There is a service to Kos in summer.
Ferries: Daily from Piraeus (via Syros and Tinos, 5½hrs), and from Rafina (via Andros and Tinos or Syros, 5hrs). Also direct from Syros (2hrs), Tinos (1hr) and Naxos. Daily in summer to Paros, Ios and Santorini. High summer express catamaran to Santorini, Syros and Iraklion.
Caique: Daily to Delos, weather permitting (½ hr).

SYROS (SIROS)
Called locally 'The Rock', Syros is mostly dry and barren, with few roads in the north, but there are hills with some greenery and beaches in the south.

◆
ERMOUPOLIS
Before the Corinth canal was cut, Ermoupolis was the most important port in Greece. Then Piraeus replaced it. But it is still centre for many Cyclades ferry routes. Passengers change ferries, often staying overnight,

so there are hotels, rooms, tavernas and some good restaurants. Its shipyards keep busy, and it makes many of those 'Greek' cotton shirts and dresses which tourists love, has tanneries and iron foundries. And it makes Loukoumia (Turkish – or Greek – delight) in many colours and flavours.

In its heyday, Ermoupolis was an elegant town. Architects from France, Italy and Germany designed houses with wrought iron balconies, fine churches, public buildings and big villas for shipowners and merchants. Its greatest splendour was the Apollo Municipal Theatre, a copy of La Scala at Milan. Until early this century, it presented an opera festival by a company from Italy. Now it is derelict. Many houses are shut because of Greek inheritance laws and family arguments. Plateia Miaoulis, the marble paved main square, is 19th-century neo-Classic with a sad faded charm, but brightens up with the evening volta when everyone walks around for hours.

◆◆
ANO SYROS (ANO SIROS)
Well worth seeing is the medieval Venetian Roman Catholic town, Ano Siros, high above the port. You can walk up the stepped streets and alleys, which takes a rewarding ¾hr, or go round the 1¼ miles (2km) by taxi. Winding, steep narrow streets criss-cross among many chapels and a Jesuit Convent founded by Louis XIII of France. In the hilltop square is St George's Cathedral and the bishop's palace.

The small resort of Finikas on the west coast has some hotels. Vari in the south is another resort with hotels and tavernas. Bus services are good.

Accommodation
Ermoupolis has plenty of choice of hotels. Smartest is the A-class **Ypatia** (tel: (0281) 23575). **Vourlis**, 5 Mavrogordatou, (tel: (0281) 28440) on the east cliff, also A-class, is in a 19th-century villa. **Hotel Europe**, 74 Stam Proiou, C-class (tel: (0281) 28771/2), has fine views.

Restaurants
Eat round Ermoupolis' main square and watch the volta.

General information
Population 19,500
Area 33 sq miles (86 sq km)
83 nautical miles from Piraeus.
Tourist Office: (tel: (0281) 26725 or 22375).
Police: just off Plateia Miaoulis (tel: (0281) 22610). Harbour Police: (tel: (0281) 22690).

How to get there
Ferries: Daily sailings from Piraeus (4¼hrs), and on to Tinos (1hr) and Mykonos (2hrs). The Mykonos route is useful, as there are daily sailings from there to Tinos, Andros and Rafina (on the mainland, 5hrs); on Sundays the ferry calls in at Syros (3½hrs to Rafina). Less frequent boats go to Naxos, Ios, Santorini, Sikinos, Folegandros, Milos, Siphnos, Serifos, Kythnos, Ikara, Samos, Iraklion (Crete), Amorgos, Donoussa and Astipalaia. There are also seasonal small ferry boats to various islands, and an express catamaran between Santorini and Crete calls in mid-summer.

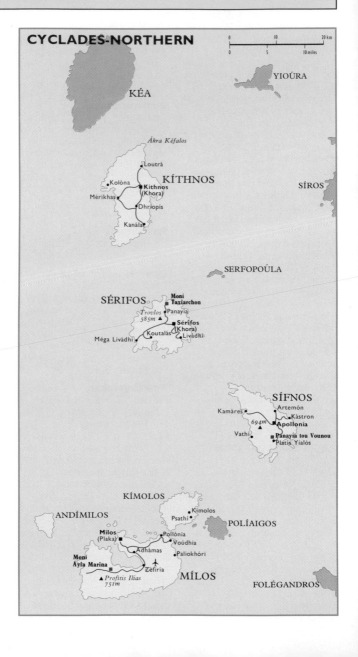

CYCLADES-NORTHERN

0   10   20 km
0   5   10 miles

YIOÚRA

KÉA

Ákra Kéfalos

Loutrá

KÍTHNOS

Kolóna
Kíthnos
(Khora)

Mérikhas

Dhriópis

SÍROS

Kanála

SERFOPOÚLA

SÉRIFOS

Moní
Taxiarchon

Troúlos
585m

Panayía

Sérifos
(Khora)

Méga Livádhi

Koutalás

Livádhi

SÍFNOS

Artemón

Kamáres

Kástron
Apollonía
694m

Vathí

Panayía tou Vounou
Platís Yialós

KÍMOLOS

ANDÍMILOS

Psathí

Kímolos

POLÍAIGOS

Mílos
(Plaka)

Pollónia
Voúdhia

Moní
Áyía Marína

Adhámas

Paliokhóri

Zefiría

Profítis Ilías
751m

MÍLOS

FOLÉGANDROS

Siphnos is a walker's island, especially if you want to go to this dramatically sited church

SIPHNOS (SIFNOS)

An enchanting island, which has the appearance of an arid mountain as you approach it. Siphnos hides its fertile valleys and carefully-cultivated terraced fields a short bus ride inland from the lively little port of Kamares.

KAMARES

Here the ferries come in, yachts come and go, fishing boats unload their catch and sell it on the quayside, weighing the lobsters as the taverna owners take their pick. The tavernas are lively and pure Greek-island. A good sandy beach stretches right round the bay.

◆◆◆
APOLLONIA

Buses regularly travel the 3½ miles (6km) to Apollonia from Kamares. The old hilltop Chora, Apollonia is so clean, freshly-whitened and neat that it looks modern until you find the narrow lanes and donkey steps of the old town, all painted white.

There are superb views over farmland to the sea from a terrace by a patisserie, where visitors and locals take coffee and wait for buses. Old churches hide in the alleys and on the hilltop is a blue-domed white church with a domed bell tower. Buses go from Apollonia past farms growing corn, olives and figs, and watch-towers built by Byzantine and Venetian rulers, to the Vrissi monastery at Exambella. Founded in 1614, it possesses precious ikons and a little museum of religious art. A left fork beyond here winds down to the fishing hamlet of Pharos (Faros), 4½ miles (7km) from Apollonia with rooms, two tavernas, and small sandy beaches. A hillside path with

Siphnos pottery makes popular, if bulky, souvenirs of the island

sea views takes you a mile (2km) from here to the monastery of Panaghia Chryssopighi on a rocky cape. Nearby is a beach taverna famous for fish.

Another bus from Apollonia takes the right fork at Exambella to Platis Yialos, a tiny resort 6 miles (10km) away. Its long beach is lined with fishermen's cottages, tavernas and bars, two hotels, rooms, and one of two official campsites on Siphnos. The other is on Kamares bay. The road back to Apollonia passes a convent, Panagia tou Vounou, with superb sea views. The nuns left last century and you can rent a cell.

◆◆◆
KASTRO (KASTRON)

The glory of Siphnos is the medieval fortified town of Kastro, set dramatically on a hillside headland over the sea, 3½ miles (5½km) by bus west from Apollonia.

Narrow whitewashed streets and alleys climb the hill, under arches of overhead houses forming bridges leading to upper floors. Pieces of ancient columns and headless busts have been used in making walls. Kastro was capital of Siphnos until 1833. It has survived through classical times, when Herodotus called it a city and it grew rich from its gold and silver mines, and through foreign occupations by Byzantines, Venetians, Franks and Turks, who held it from 1617 to 1834. In classical times Siphnos was one of the biggest contributors to the treasure of the oracle at Delphi, sending each year a golden egg. One year the islanders sent a stone wrapped in gold leaf. The gods showed their wrath by sinking the mines beneath the sea. The island became known for pottery, and potters still work in Kamares, Vathy and Apollonia. Over the mountain from Kastro is the 16th-century Chrysostomou monastery, centre of resistance to the Turks. Siphnos is short of roads or even driveable mule tracks. Nice bays on the west coast can be reached only by hard walking over mountains, or by boat. Caiques go in summer to Vathy, which has a fishing harbour, a sandy beach in a horseshoe bay, a 16th-century church, two tavernas and rooms. Siphnos is a 'connoisseur's' island.

Accommodation

Kamares: **Stavros**, on the quayside (tel: (0284) 31641) is C-class, very friendly, simple and convenient, but the rooms vary a lot. Apollonia: **Sofia**, round the corner from the patisserie, is a good C-class hotel, with restaurant (tel: (0284) 31238). **Anthoussa**, over the patisserie, is modern with lovely views, C-class, book early (tel: (0284) 31431). **Hotel Sifnos,** Katarati, up the lane opposite the police station (Odhos Stylianou Prokou) is C-class (tel: (0284) 31624). Platis Yialos: **Hotel Platis Yialos**, B-class, clean and comfortable, opens only in summer and you need to book (tel: (0284) 31324).

Restaurants

Tavernas on Kamares waterfront are great fun. Apollonia has a good choice of eating places. The simple taverna next to the patisserie has good cooking and views from its terrace. **Restaurant Cyprus** on the main museum square is smarter and more formal. **Restaurant Krevatina**, in a charming tiny square uphill from the police station, has the most variety of dishes, well-cooked, but closes around 14.00hrs until evening. In Kastro, **Zorba's** taverna has fair food.

General information

Population 2,100
Area 32 sq miles (82 sq km)
76 nautical miles from Piraeus.
Police: in Apollonia, in an alley off museum square.
Tourist Police: (tel: (0284) 31210).
Harbour Police: in Kamares (tel: (0284) 31617).

How to get there

Ferries: Important small excursion boats (no cars) go to Paros, where you can pick up boats to other islands: daily, June–September; 2 or 3 times a week in spring and autumn.
Car Ferries: 4 days a week from Piraeus (via Kythnos and Seriphos, 6hrs), and on to Kimolos and Milos; weekly to Folegandros, Sikinos, Ios and Santorini. Also a connection with Syros.

SERIPHOS (SERIFOS)

Seriphos has never been a tourist island, which makes it particularly attractive to the travellers who do go. At the centre is a mountain, Trovlos, reaching 1,919 ft (585m). Much of the isle is bare rock.
The main paved road zig-zags 1¾ miles (3km) up to Khora (Serifos Town), the old fortified town. Other roads are rough but driveable – but hire cars are scarce. There are several taxis. You can sometimes get lifts on supply trucks. Two buses run only between the port of Livadi and Khora. The best way to the beaches is by caique.

LIVADI (LIVADHI)

Set in a biggish near-horseshoe bay among hills, Livadi is a working fishing port, with the ferry pier and enough tavernas, shops, pensions and rooms to cater for a few tourists and for the yachtsmen who have discovered it. It is a friendly, happy little place, where you can just sit and talk for hours. The slow pace leaves time for thinking, dreaming, reading and resting. There is a beach round the bay, but better ones nearby.

CYCLADES

Livakadia beach, reached by a track over a hill behind the ferry quay, is sandy, narrow and treelined, with a surf-riding school in mid-summer. Another half-hour's walk takes you to Karavi beach, which is fairly empty but has some hillside holiday homes. By following the river bed (dry in summer) over a hill you reach Psili Amos, a lovely sandy cove with dunes. In another 15 minutes you reach Aghios Giannis, which is larger but has coarser sand.

◆◆
KHORA (SERIFOS TOWN)
The old capital, Khora, a mile (2km) from Livadi, looks spectacular from the port. As well as taking a bus or taxi, you can climb to it up steep wide donkey-steps; the walk down is more fun. To reach the older part of Khora, you climb steps from the bus-stop square, side-stepping laden mules. You

The best way to see old villages and landscapes on Seriphos is to walk

reach a marble-paved square with a charming church and a large 1908 town hall with iron railings of sculpted swans. Steps spiral up to a crumbling Venetian fort where the whole island population could take refuge from Turkish pirates. A mile past Khora the road divides. The right hand road, with fine sea views, divides again after the village of Panayia (with a 10th-century Byzantine church) into two rough tracks, dangerous for mopeds. The left leads to a good sandy beach at Sikamia, 4 miles (6km) from Khora with dunes, clear clean sea and a few buildings. The right track leads to Taxiarchon monastery (Moní Taxiarchon), built in 1600, fortified and painted white with a red dome. It contains Byzantine manuscripts and good 18th-century frescos. A track leads to a pretty village, Kallistos, with a restaurant. The left hand fork on the Khora road also divides. The right

track goes to the old iron and copper mining village of Mega Livadi, 4½ miles (7km) from Khora, with ruined buildings, a broad sandy beach and a hamlet with a taverna. The left track leads to Koutalas, a big bay with a shingle shore, a few houses on the back slopes, fishing boats and a taverna. Signs of prehistoric settlement were found in a nearby cave. Legend has it that the rocks of Seriphos used to be the people. The Greek hero Perseus and his mother Danaë landed here after being set adrift in a box. Lecherous King Polydeuces wanted Danaë badly, so he got rid of young Perseus by tricking him into promising to get for him the head of the gorgon Medusa whose bulging eyes turned men to stone. The goddess Athena gave Perseus a mirror-like shield, winged shoes for quick escape and a cloak which made him invisible. Returning with the head in a sack, he turned the King and his whole court to stone.

Accommodation

Livadi: **Serifos Beach**, Paralia (in a cul-de-sac off the quayside) is the best, run by Austrians; book (tel: (0281) 51209), C-class. **Perseus** (B-class pension) along the seafront, is beside restaurant Perseus (tel: (0281) 51273). **Maistrali**, C-class, is just past Perseus (tel: (0281) 51381).

Restaurants

The best tavernas are in the port. Recommended are the restaurant next to the Rock Cocktail Bar, the **Perseus** (over the river bridge) and the

International on the way to the ferry-boat quay.

General information

Population 1,100
Area 27 sq miles (70 sq km)
70 nautical miles from Piraeus.
Tourist Police: (tel: (0281) 51300).
Harbour Police: on the Chora road (tel: (0281) 51470).

How to get there

Ferries: 4 days a week from Piraeus (via Kythnos, 5hrs), and on to Siphnos, Kimolos and Milos; weekly to Folegandros, Sikinos, Ios and Santorini. There is also a connection with Syros. In season, some boats go to Paros, but otherwise you must change at Siphnos.

KYTHNOS (KITHNOS)

A few knowledgeable tourists have visited Kythnos for many years for one reason – the waters of the spa of Loutra. Those who do go are nearly all Greeks, and there are still very few others. Locals still totally outnumber visitors even in mid-summer in the fishing port of Merikhas, although more yachtsmen now explore these three lesser-known and attractive isles of the Cyclades – Syphnos, Seriphos and Kythnos – rather than the more-crowded isles. The result is that Kythnos tavernas and hotels are simple and cheap: people seem quite ashamed to take your money. Water can be scarce by the end of the summer.
Buses run in the old Greek Island way – more often by whim than timetable. The best way to get around Kythnos is by shared taxi. Helpful drivers.

LOUTRA

Loutra, 5 miles (8km) from
Merikhas, has a faded charm
despite a new apartment block
and a new hotel, and shops are
being built. It looks 'ripe for
development'. There is already
the bungalow-style Xenia-
Anagenissis Hotel, with two
streams of water running
alongside which are brown
from iron deposits. One runs at
precisely 37°C (99°F) and is
used for drinking. The other at
52°C (126°F) is for bathing.
They are said to alleviate
rheumatism and promote
fertility. The spring is under a
church next to the baths.
Loutra is still a fishing port, with
boats alongside the quay below
a church, a tiny castle which is
now somebody's summer
home, and rusting iron-mining
gear. Over the sands before the
quay are simple but lively
tavernas.

KHORA (KITHNOS TOWN)

A modern road from the spa
winds up 2 miles (3km) among
fertile land towards Khora, the
old capital, then down 3 miles
(5km) more to Merikhas, but
you are as likely to see farmers
riding donkeys side-saddle as
cars. Kythnos is essentially an
old-style agricultural island.
Khora has old white buildings
and useful shops, the post
office, and a restaurant. But it is
dull and has no hotel.

MERIKHAS

A very pleasant and genuine
fishing port. Tavernas have
tables on the esplanade above
a tree-lined but unattractive
beach of greyish coarse sand.
Ten minutes walk from the port
is a very fertile valley leading to
a long narrow cove with coarse
sand, called Kolona. It has a
taverna and you can walk
across a strip of sand to a tiny
island. Unfortunately there is
some unofficial camping here,
with its usual problems of
sanitation and litter. You can
reach Kolona by water taxi.
The only other road climbs 2½
miles (4km) from Merikhas with
fine views to the delightful
hillside town of Driopis, which
has narrow, weaving streets
and donkey steps with old
shops, houses and a few little
tavernas. Sudden views appear
around corners. You can walk
from here to Katafiki cave.
The road continues (and so do
occasional buses) 2½ miles
(4km) downhill to Kanala, a
well-kept little modern resort,
with trees to give shade from
the noon-day sun and rich in
flowers. The fishing boat quay
is used also by a few yachts and
over a hill is a narrow gritty-
sand beach. Here are a
pension, rooms, and a café-bar
and taverna serving good
standard Greek dishes. A
relaxing hideout. A monastery
here has an ikon said to have
been painted by St Luke.
Several sandy coves round the
isle can be reached by boat or
on foot, some from Merikhas. S
Stephano beach can be
reached from Driopis.

Accommodation
Loutra: **Xenia-Anagenissis**, C-
class, is the island's best hotel;
open June–October; usually

booked up mid-summer (tel: (0281) 31217). Merikhas **Kythnos** (up steps from the fishing quay) is small, modern, clean and very friendly (tel: (0281) 31247). **Possidonion**, C-class, at the end of the esplanade, is big (6-storey); many rooms are booked mid-summer by Austrian package tours (tel: (0281) 32100).

Restaurants
In Loutra, the beach tavernas are good, amusing and good value. In Merikhas there is nothing very good, but **O'Antonis** restaurant in a cul-de-sac opposite the bus-stop has variety and is friendly. The **Porto-Bello** on the esplanade often has lobster or other good fish, and the **Gialos** restaurant next door is considered the smartest eating place.

General information
Population 1,500
Area 33 sq miles (86 sq km)
52 nautical miles from Piraeus.
Tourist Police: (tel: (0281) 31201). Harbour Police: (tel: (0281) 31290).

How to get there
Ferries: From Piraeus 4 days a week (4hrs); Lavrio also on the mainland (via Kea) weekly (4hrs); Seriphos, Siphnos, Kimolos and Milos 4 days a week; weekly to Foleqandros, Sikinos, Ios and Santorini. There is also a connection with Syros.

MILOS
Milos can be disappointing. The approach into the vast Bay of Adamas between little islets, past fishing hamlets and an inviting, sandy headland to the quay of Adamas village is almost idyllic.

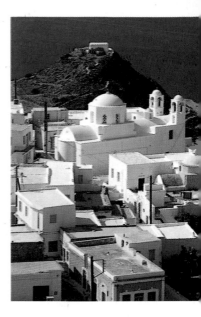

A sparkling white church in Milos

But the countryside inland is gashed by the mines and quarries which made Milos rich from antiquity.

◆
ADAMAS (ADHAMAS)
The little port, in a ring of hills, is pretty, with little yachts flying flags of many nations coming and going through Adamas Bay, but big enough to hold the whole Allied Fleet of these seas in World War I. But the port can be stifling and dusty from the mineral ores brought here for shipment. Most tourists stay in hotels along nearby Lanada beach. The island in the bay, Anti Milos, is a sanctuary for chamois and beyond it are odd rock formations, such as 'the bears' (Arkoudes).

CYCLADES

PLAKA (MILOS TOWN)

The capital, where most islanders live in winter because of flooding, is a short bus-ride up the hill from Adamas. It has two museums. The History and Folk Museum contains interesting relics of island life. The Archaeological Museum has some of the finds from Milos going back to the Neolithic Age (08.30–15.00hrs; closed Monday). Plaka is believed to be on the site of ancient Melos, which was destroyed in revenge by the Athenians after the wars with the Spartans whom Melos supported. The men of Melos were killed, women and children enslaved and replaced by Athenian colonists. At the village of Tripiti near Plaka in 1890 British archaeologists unearthed catacombs dating from the island's conversion to Christianity in the 1st century AD. The bones in the arched tombs turned to dust when the caves were opened, so now they are closed again. The Roman theatre is partly unexcavated. Nearby is the spot where in 1820 a farmer found a cave with a 2nd century statue of Aphrodite, goddess of love and fertility (Venus to the Romans). The Greeks say that, to save her from the Turks, they lent her to the French for safe keeping. In a scuffle between islanders and the French Navy, she lost her pedestal and arms. The Venus of Milos (*Venus de Milo*) is now in the Louvre in Paris ('Purchased' say the French, 'Stolen', say the islanders). The museum in Plaka has only a plaster cast.

◆ ZEPHIRIA (ZEFIRIA)

Buses from Plaka go past Adamas along the coast where there are places to swim, then turn inland at an electric power station among mines and machinery to Zephiria, 7 miles (11km) away and capital from the 8th century until 1793. Once it had 5,000 people, 17 churches and two bishops. Pestilence from pirate ships and sulphur fumes from the mines drove out the people.

A rough road used, surprisingly, by buses runs from Zephiria over the hills to Paliochori, 10 miles (16km) from Plaka, a beach of grey volcanic sand with several tavernas and a restaurant. The coast road from the power station passes several sandy beaches. The road itself climbs to Aghia Marina (Moní Áyia Marina) monastery on the side of Mount Profitis Elias. Two beaches north – Phatourena, by a lagoon, and Emborio, can be reached only by boat.

One of the most attractive places on Milos is the little fishing port of Pollonia in the north, 6 miles (9.5km) from Adamas port and reached by bus. It has Greek holiday homes, rooms to let, tavernas and restaurants, and a sandy beach. From here you can get a caique to the isle of Kimolos (½hr).

Accommodation

Adamas: **Meltemi**, C-class; near bus square (tel: (0287) 22284). **Venus Village** is a large, B-class hotel-bungalow complex (tel: (0287) 22030). **Semiramis** on the waterfront round the bay, is pretty; D-class, but most rooms

have wc-shower (tel: (0287)
22117/8).

Restaurants
The best places to eat are in
Adamas. **Aphroditis** serves fine
sea food and the **Charcoal
Taverna** is good value.

General information
Population 5,000
Area 62 sq miles (160 sq km)
82 nautical miles from Piraeus.
Tourist Police: (tel: (0287)
21378).
Harbour Police: (tel: (0287)
22100).

How to get there
Ferries: From Piraeus: direct 4
days a week, also 4 days a
week via Kythnos, Seriphos,
Siphnos and Kimolos (8hrs);
weekly to Folegandros, Sikinos,
Ios and Santorini; Iraklion
(Crete) 3 days a week. There is
a caique to Paros, July–August.

PAROS
Paros was near-paradise to
knowledgeable travellers 20
years ago: a lively place, with
an important little shipping port
for inter-island trading, two
busy fishing ports, yachts
calling but few other tourists.
The big sand beaches across
the isle were empty, the farms
prosperous. Inevitably it has
been discovered. There are
four or five middle-sized
package hotels, an airfield
linked with Athens and Crete,
and more ferries from Piraeus.
But it remains delightful, though
Parikia port and the fishing
village of Naousa are
overcrowded in mid-summer.
So are buses. Although bus
services are good, a hire-car
can be very useful.

*Piso Livadi is a lively fishing port
and resort on Paros*

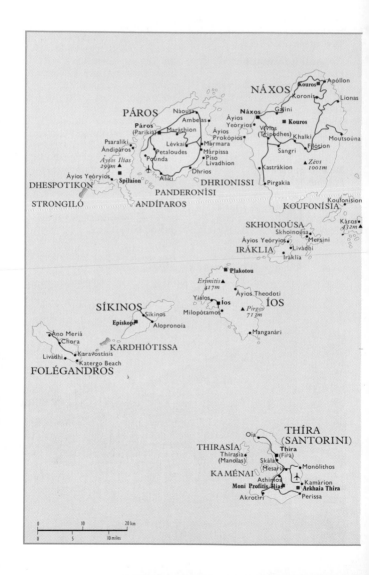

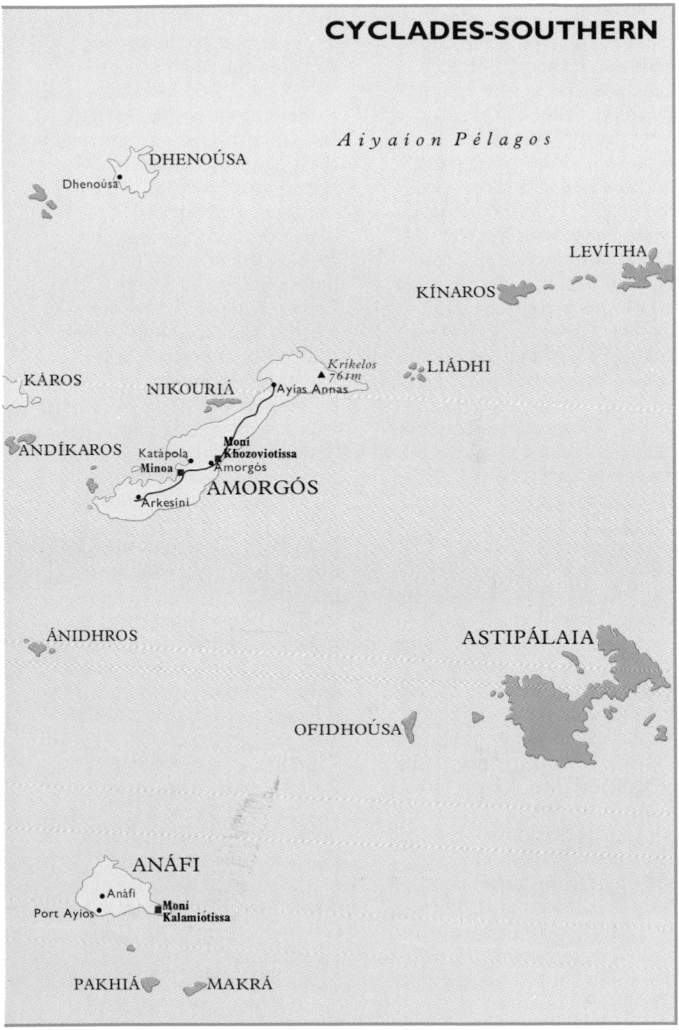

CYCLADES-SOUTHERN

Aiyaion Pélagos

DHENOÚSA

Dhenoúsa

LEVÍTHA

KÍNAROS

KÁROS

NIKOURIÁ

Krikelos
▲ *761m*

LIÁDHI

Ayías Ánnas

ANDÍKAROS

Katápola

Moní
Khozoviótissa

Minoa

Amorgós

AMORGÓS

Arkesíni

ÁNIDHROS

ASTIPÁLAIA

OFIDHOÚSA

ANÁFI

Anáfi

Moní
Kalamiótissa

Port Ayiós

PAKHIÁ

MAKRÁ

CYCLADES

♦♦
PARIKIA (PAROS TOWN)

The quayside at Parikia where the ferries dock is a working port, and the main square, Plateia Mavrogenous, behind it is a business centre, with banks, offices and tavernas crowded with visitors in the evenings. Off it runs the narrow old High Street, Lochagou Kortianou, with every sort of little shop.

A maze of white-painted lanes and alleys with donkey-steps leads off the High Street, with white houses adorned with flower boxes, churches, and open workshops where men make shoes, furniture and clothes. On a hillock are the ruins of a Venetian fort built in 1260 using Doric columns from a Greek temple. You reach finally an esplanade lined with tavernas and cafés, and a tree-lined beach of sand and shingle with a wind-surfing school.

In the town are three 18th-century marble fountains. The pride of Paros is the Ekatontapyliani – the 'church of one hundred doors'. It was designed in the 6th century for the Emperor Justinian by Ignatius, apprentice to Isadore of Miletus, architect of St Sophia's in Constantinople (Istanbul). Ignatius designed it so well that Isadore was jealous and tried to push him off the roof. In the tussle, they both fell. They are commemorated by sculpture at the base of a column in the courtyard. It is said that 99 doors from the church have been found and that when the 100th is found the Greeks will recover Constantinople.

Damaged by an earthquake in 1773, the church was restored in the 1960s to its original Byzantine design in the form of a cross. Its bell tower was destroyed in the earthquake, so the bell hangs now from a huge cypress tree. In the National Archaeological Museum (08.30–14.00hrs; closed Mondays) next to the church, is a sadly-small section of the Parian Chronicle (Marmor Parium), a social history of Greece carved in Parian marble from 265BC and discovered in the early 17th century. Much more of it is in the Ashmolean Museum in Oxford (England). There is also a frieze and biography of the satirical poet Archilochos, who invented the iambic pentameter as the best way of delivering his witty blasts at authority.

Parian marble made the island rich. It was used by Pericles to build the Acropolis in Athens, for the Temple of Solomon in Jerusalem and for the Venus de Milo. The old quarries at Marathi, 3 miles (5km) from Parikia, became uneconomic but were revived in 1844 to supply marble for Napoleon's tomb. You can visit the quarries, but take a light and a sweater. The longest tunnel – 295ft (90m) – is dark, cold and damp. Near the medieval capital of Lefkas in the centre of the isle, 5½ miles (9km) from Parikia, the village of Marmara has streets paved with marble. Marpissa, half a mile (1km) from Marmara, is the prettiest village here. Above its windmills are ruins of a 15th-century Venetian fortress and the 16th-century monastery Aghios Antonios.

◆◆◆
NAOUSA

Naousa, the fishing port 7½ miles (12km) north of Parikia, is no longer peaceful and idyllic but is delightful. In the little working port where fishing boats are packed tight against the seawall you can eat fish taken literally from boats to the pan. Little hotels and small low apartments have been built recently, but in the network of little streets off the square houses are typically Cycladic. Several little beaches are within walking distance of Naousa.

Ambelas, a fishing village on the east coast, 3 miles (5km) from Naousa, has a beach and is becoming a small resort with hotels.

Piso Livadi, 13 miles (21km) from Parikia across the island, is a pleasant, lively fishing port and resort in summer, almost deserted in winter. The quay and beach are backed by tavernas and little hotels, South from here along the coast are five beaches which you can walk along. There is a bus, usually crowded. Logaros beach has lovely sands and tavernas. Chrysi Akti has long golden sands and is the best beach on the island. Dryos, where the bus turns back, is an old fruit-growing village turned into a posh little resort where Athenians have summer villas. Several beaches beyond are often deserted.

◆
ALYKI (ALIKI)

Through beautiful farmland above seascapes you reach Alyki, joined to Parikia 7½ miles

The ever-popular 'Greek' salad for lunch at a taverna in the inner harbour, Naousa

(12km) away by a paved road. A fishing village with a lovely tree-lined sandy beach, it is growing fast, with hotels, tavernas, several restaurants, a disco and cement-block villas built by Athenians. The airport is here, with direct flights to Athens, and it is expanding to take bigger planes.

◆
POUNTA (POUNDA)

The road runs on to Pounta (Punta), a little village with a good hotel, bars, tavernas and a big quay, 6¼ miles (10km) from Parikia. Little ferries shuttle between here and the small isle of Antiparos (see page 43) a 10 minute journey. Yachtsmen should beware – currents are strong, winds tricky.

CYCLADES

The lush valley Petaloudes behind Pounta, with its thick woods and constantly-running stream, is known as the Valley of Butterflies.
Try to avoid July and August in Paros. In other months it is charming.

Accommodation

Lefkas: has a big **Xenia Hotel** with lovely views, bar and restaurant, but it is not in a convenient spot, B-class (tel: (0284) 21394). Parikia: **Georgy**, Plateia Mavrogenous, central; rooms with wc, shower (tel: (0284) 21667), C-class. **Dina**, just off Plateia Velentza by Aghios Triada Church, E-class but charming with garden (tel: (0284) 21325). Naousa: **Hotel Aliprantis**, C-class, excellent position on main square, rooms with wc, shower (tel: (0284) 51571). **Minoa**, Aghios Panteleimonou (south end of town), C-class, rooms with balconies, good restaurant (tel: (0284) 51309). Aghios Argiti, ½ mile (1km) from Naousa: **Calypso**, overlooking sandy beach, C-class (tel: (0284) 51488). Piso Livadi: **Marpissa**, B-class pension, (tel: (0284) 41288). **Leto**, C-class (tel: (0284) 41283).
Campsites: Koula (at Parikia), open April to October; restaurant, supermarket, showers (tel: (0284) 22081/2). Capt. Cafkis Camping (at Piso Livadi); pool, supermarket, café (tel: (0284) 41392/5).

Restaurants

Parikia: **To Tamarisko**, Odhos Agorakritou, is still probably the best on the island. **Kriako's** High Street, is good and pricey.

Limanaki is probably best of those along the tourist beach southwest of the ferry quay, with good fish. **Restaurant Argonauta** beside the Bank of Commerce in Mavrogenous Square, serves good dishes. Above is a good value clean hotel (rooms with wc and shower) but often full. Naousa: there are very good seafood tavernas by the harbour. **Christos Taverna** at the top of the High Street is excellent.

General information

Population 8,000
Area 81 sq miles (209 sq km)
95 nautical miles from Piraeus.
Tourist Office: (tel: (0284) 22679).
Tourist Police: 24 Plateia Mavrogenous (tel: (0284) 21673).
Harbour Police: (tel: (0284) 21240).

How to get there

Air: Two flights daily from Athens, more in July–August (50mins). To Iraklion (Crete) 1 May–September, 3 days a week (45mins); Rhodes 4 days a week (1hr 10 mins).
Ferries: From Piraeus 1–3 sailings daily May-September, 5 days a week in winter (7hrs). 'No-car' ferry to Siphnos daily, useful also for changing ferries to Seriphos, Kythnos and other isles. Daily ferries to Ios, Santorini and Naxos. Other ferries to Amorgos, (5 days a week), Astypalaia, Ikara, Iraklia, Shinoussa, Koufonissi, Mykonos (all 3 days a week), Folegandros, Sikinos, Kalimnos, Kos, Nisiros, Tilos, Symi, Rhodes, Crete, Karpathos, Kasos, Syros and Donoussa (once a week). Also many excursion boats in summer.

The clear water of the fishing harbour, Antiparos

ANTIPAROS (ANDIPAROS)

Until recently, people went to Antiparos almost entirely to look at the cave at Spileon. Now back-packers in particular go for the near-deserted beaches and clear waters. No cars are allowed, although mopeds are on hire in mid-summer – a noisy hazard. The tree-lined harbour, with a windmill (now a disco), and white fishermen's chapel, has beautifully clear water. It is a 5 minute walk from the only real settlement, the attractive old Venetian fortified town of Kastro, and nearly all the tavernas, restaurants, shops, hotels and cafés are on the quay, in the town or along the connecting road.

◆◆
SPILEON (SPILAION)

The only road goes to Spileon, a 2-hour thirsty tramp. But you can get a caique from the ferry quay most of the year.

The cave entrance is a half-hour's slog up the slopes of Mount Aghios Ilias, which rises to 751ft (229m). But teams of mules await to give you a ride – pricey but well worth it. The entrance is by a church. Once visitors went down and up by rope. Now there are 400 cement steps. The cave is dark, dripping, cold and eerie. Stalactites and stalagmites up to 10ft (3m) long have survived centuries of looting by souvenir hunters, graffiti writers and even German hand grenades in 1941-45. Refugees have hidden in this cave since men fled here from the wrath of the Macedonian Alexander the Great.

A graffiti inscription in Latin records a Christmas Mass celebrated here in 1673 for the French Ambassador to Constantinople, Count Nouantelle, who paid 500 Parians and Antiparians to attend. A true eccentric, he then had Christmas dinner aboard the pirate-ship of Daniel of Malta.

Accommodation
Chryssi Akti on the Kastro beach is elegant and the best hotel, C-class (tel: (0284) 61206). **Mantalena**, Kastro, D-class has some rooms with wc, showers (tel: (0284) 61220).

Restaurants
Antiparos is not very good for eating. **Yorgos** taverna in Kastro is the most popular.

General information
Population 650
Area 13½ sq miles (35 sq km)
Tourist Office & Tourist Police: Kastro (tel: (0284) 61202).

How to get there
Ferries: Taxi-ferry from Pounta on Paros (10mins). Summer caiques 1–3 daily from Parikia, Paros (40mins).

NAXOS ✓

Biggest of the Cyclades, Naxos has been blessed by nature. Its mountains are greener and more beautiful than the rugged mountains of Crete. Even when the mountain rivers and waterfalls run dry in summer, they are a riot of oleander flowers. The green fertile plains produce lemons, olives, nuts, grapes, flowers and vegetables. Its beaches are superb.
Bus services are not bad, but a good way of getting around Naxos in summer is to hire a mini-moke. Closed cars can be too hot, and scooters are dangerous on the dirt roads.

◆
NAXOS (KHORA)
The port and capital, Naxos is a working town, putting tourism and beauty second to commerce. The narrow streets of the medieval town uphill from the harbour are dark and can look sinister. Within the walls of the old Khora are Venetian houses, doorways and coats-of-arms, and on the hilltop sit a Venetian kastro, a Ducal palace and other Italian palazzi. An Italian freebooter, Marco Sanuda, took the isle in 1207, became Duke of Naxos and ruler of several Cycladian isles.
The harbour has plenty of tavernas, bars, restaurants and shops around it. From here they export wine, olive oil, grain and figs. The lemon trade has died off, but they make a sweet and sour liqueur called Kitrou from lemon leaves – four varieties and colours from slightly to very sweet. The people of Naxos make above average wines, too (Promponas red, rosé and white are palatable, Ariadne better). And so they should, for Dionysus (Bacchus, god of wine) taught them. He sailed in one fine day to find Ariadne, daughter of King Minos of Crete, lying asleep on a beach. She had fled with Theseus after helping him slay the Minotaur in the maze, but he abandoned her on Naxos while she slept, sailing sneakily for Athens. But Dionysus found the sunbathing beauty and seduced her. A festival dedicated to Dionysus is held in mid-August in Naxos's main square.
The one Classical Greek touch in the port is an 18ft-high (5.5m) marble doorway on an islet joined by a causeway – all that remains of a temple of Apollo begun in 522BC and never finished.

Aghios Georgios beach, long, with dunes, is almost a suburb of Naxos, with hotels, bars and discos. Aghia Anna can be reached by bus or caique, so is also popular. A 15-minute walk north from here is the quieter Aghios Prokopios. All these beaches have rooms, so has Kastraki, south by an unpaved road, with a hamlet and beach taverna. South from here, with a paved road back to Naxos, is Pirgaki, with a fine sand beach. The Pirgaki-Naxos road goes through Sangri, 6 miles (10km) from Naxos, hamlets of old houses in cobbled streets encircled by castles, windmills and ruined by Byzantine and Venetian villas. A left road leads to Tripodos (Vivlos), a large, attractive village where wine is produced. Nearby is Aghios Mamos, a recently restored 8th-century cathedral with remarkable 7th-century ikons. The other road from Sangri goes through attractive country to Chalki (Khalki), 10 miles (16km) from Naxos, a pretty village, centre for old Venetian castles and Byzantine churches. The route becomes spectacular, with gorgeous mountain views, to Filoti, largest village on the island, on the slopes of Mount Zia (Zeus). The road zig-zags to high villages, and you can take a truly rough snaking road to Moutsouna, an old east-coast port with a shingle beach, taverna and old sheds. The main road snakes north through the mountains to the highest village Koronida (Koronis), pretty with lovely views of woods, fields and mountain streams, then drops down to the delightful fishing port of Apollonia 18½ miles (30km) from Naxos.

The attractive waterfront at Naxos is lined with bars, tavernas, restaurants, shops and hotels

APOLLONIA (APOLLON)
This village is still typically
'Greek-island', with fishing
caiques slapping against the
quayside, tavernas on the quay
road, houses and hotels on the
shingle beach beyond rocks;
no-one hurrying, everyone
finding time for a chat or an
ouzo. But in high summer
excursion coaches now arrive
from Naxos, so it is at its best
before mid-day or in the
evening, when the far from
serious business of eating and
drinking begins in the tavernas.
While the excursionists are
there, you can walk to sandy
coves or to the old marble
quarries to see the Kouros, a
sculpted figure of a man 34½ft
(10.5m) high made around
650BC, but uncompleted.
You can see better but smaller
Kouroi ('young men') at Flerio, 3
miles (5km) northeast of Naxos.
They are 16½ft (5m) tall, are
marching with their arms down
and may have been guardians of
Zeus, father of the gods.
From Apollonia runs a rough
coastal road round the north
and west coasts, with
spectacular scenery. A series of
attractive coves begins with
Ormos Abram, a farming village
by a pebble beach, with a
pension. Other beaches include
Chilia Voyssi, with tracks to two
coves, and Galini, where a
valley path leads to an attractive
cove. From here the road to
Naxos is paved.

Accommodation
There are plenty of hotels,
pensions and rooms in Naxos
and at nearby beaches. In
Naxos, the **Ariadne**, 1 Ariadnis
Street, is a B-class pension with
fine harbour views (tel: (0285)
22452). **Panorama**, Amphitritis
Kastro, C-class, has super sea
views and some rooms with WC,
shower (tel: (0285) 22330).

Restaurants
There is plenty of choice,
especially in Naxos and at
Aghios Georgios beach, of
places to eat. **Taverna
Karvagio** on Paralia Ariadnis
has a wide choice of good
dishes. **Meltemi Restaurant**
close to it is a favourite.

General information
Population 14,000
Area 173 sq miles (448 sq km)
106 nautical miles from Piraeus.
Tourist Office & Tourist Police:
in Naxos (tel: (0285) 22100).
Harbour Police: (tel: (0285)
22300).

How to get there
Ferries: From Piraeus (via
Paros) 2 sailings most days
(8hrs); from Ios and Santorini
1–2 sailings a day; from
Mykonos (non-car vessel) 4
days a week; from Rafina daily
(6½hrs). Other ferries go on
various days to Iraklion (Crete),
Shinoussa, Koufonissi,
Donoussa, Amorgos, Syros and
Astipalaia. A little motor vessel
(no cars) goes twice a week to
Crete, Donoussa and Amorgos.

IOS
The little isle of Ios, once
peaceful and idyllic, has gone
through the sound barrier in a
few years. It is still a delight to
the young who worship sun,
sand, sex, souvlaki and sound. If
you value peace, do not go to Ios
between Easter and September.

Ios has a little port, Gialos, a startlingly white, old town (Chora) with dozens of little domed churches amid alleyways and steep lanes, reached from the port by a paved road or steep mule track, and superb beaches. There are also a mass of tourist shops and disco bars belting out loud rhythms until dawn. The crowds have brought an acute water shortage, affecting sewerage.

◆
MILOPOTAMOS
The excellent Milopotamos beach, deserted not long ago, has restaurants, cafés, bars, two campsites, several small hotels and a supermarket. Here most of the young sleep until early evening, so that it is difficult not to tread on them if you want to reach the water.

Buses from the port to the Chora now continue to this beach. Invasions started with the arrival of the flower children in the late 1960s. They were friendly, peaceful and broke, so that they slept on the beach, but caused no trouble. There was one disco in a deserted windmill and classical music at the Ios Club. By the mid-1970s you could smell the marijuana as you landed. Ios was over-run with young people, many of them hippies. Beaches were fouled, litter accumulated, mosquitoes and flies multiplied, drugs brought thievery and fights. Not unnaturally, the police got tough. They stopped beach-sleeping, and put hippies on return boats.

Now most visitors are young people who have money for

An Ios local in traditional costume

beds and food. They have a wonderful time dancing until dawn and sleeping by day. The great awakening comes in early evening as they wander into bars for their first drink or to their rooms for a shower before the evening action. It is the nightly noise which drives away the older devotees of Ios.

Less crowded than Milopotamos bay is the big sandy Aghios Theodotis beach 6 miles (10km) across the island, but it is getting more popular. A rough road leads to it, but it takes 3 hours to walk. A bus runs once a day in summer. It has a taverna , rooms of what are called 'Indian Huts', which are the stone huts of a long-forgotten attempt to set up a sort of Club Méditerranée here. You can reach Manganari beach in the south only by boat from the port (50 minutes each way). Here there are two tavernas and a fairly pricey German built hotel with restaurant and disco. There is little to see on Ios, and no transport except buses and walking. Above Aghios Theodotis beach are the ruins of a Venetian medieval fortress and a monastery where the people hid from pirates. Homer died on Ios, and enthusiasts go by donkey or on foot (2–3hrs) to Plakotos in the north, on the slopes of Mount Erimitis, where his tomb was said to be.

SIKINOS

Two ferries a week from Piraeus to Ios call at the nearby island of Sikinos, and there are some boat excursions from Ios in summer. It is a very simple isle, living from land and sea, with mules and donkeys doing the fetching and carrying. There are no cars or buses yet. It has a delightful Chora and deserted beaches in the south.

Accommodation

Nissos Ios, on Milopotamos beach, D-class (tel: (0286) 91306). **Delfini**, Milopotamos beach, is more civilised than most, C-class (tel: (0286) 91340/1). **Aktaeon**, over Acteon Travel office on port square, D-class (tel: (0286) 91207). **Armadoros**, smart C-class (tel: (0286) 91201). **Sea Breeze** (Thalasia Avra), in a small lane by Acteon Travel, is popular from old days, C-class (tel: (0286) 91285). Chora: **Afroditi** on beach road, good D-class (tel: (0286) 91546).

Restaurants

Simple, but best for food, is probably **Draco's Taverna** (*not* Dracos Restaurant) by Milopotamos beach, noted for fish (pricey on Ios). It is also a pension (tel: (0286) 91243).

General information

Population 1,450
Area 41½ sq miles (108 sq km)
107 nautical miles from Piraeus.
Tourist Office & Tourist Police: Town Hall, Chora (tel: (0286) 91222).
Harbour police: (tel: (0286) 91264).

How to get there

Ferries: Almost daily from Piraeus in summer, 2–3 times a week in winter (11hrs); daily to Santorini, Naxos (3hrs) and Paros (5hrs); 2 times a week to Sikinos, Folegandros and Siphnos; twice a week to Seriphos and Syros (1hr); once a week to Tinos and Milos. Small boats go to Sikinos (45mins).

SANTORINI (THIRA, THERA)

Santorini is spectacular, dramatic, not very loveable and sinister to some visitors. But it is interesting. Crescent shaped, it is the surviving land of a volcanic eruption of around 1600BC which sunk the rest of the isle in the bay, leaving three smaller isles, two of which (Kameni isles) are still actively volcanic. The tidal wave from the eruption is believed to have destroyed the Minoan cities of Crete. Smaller eruptions have followed through the centuries, the last in 1956. Much of the isle is covered with pumice and lava, and beaches are of 'black' (grey) volcanic dust.

THIRA

The town of Thira (Thera or Fira), spread along a cliff above the old ferry port, Skala, is very attractive, despite being almost totally rebuilt after the 1956 earthquake. Exploring the town in daytime is purgatory. Most shops sell souvenirs or tourist clothes and fanatical sales touts not only pester you but almost drag you into their shops. Restaurants hurry you through meals, too, as if they need your table. The reason is that cruise ships and excursions from other isles pour their passengers into the town all day. After the shops shut, you can admire Thira – a white cubist town on terraces,

Startlingly white modern churches rise up on terraces above Thira

with pretty churches between houses. Views are superb, and restaurants are sited so that you can eat and admire them. For superb views and good food, eat at Leschis. When excursion boats cease in October, Thira shuts down until early May. Winters are terrible on Santorini. Gales and fierce seas can cut it off, even by air. The Archaeological Museum has vases and jars excavated at Ancient Thira and Akrotiri, and Roman sculptures (08.30–15.00hrs; closed Mondays). In the Orthodox cathedral is a museum of ecclesiastical relics. Happily there is now a cable car up the cliff from Skala to Thira. The cliff is 886ft (270m) high with 587 steps. You can still go up the old way, by mule, but the muleteers must be some of the

nastiest people in the Greek
Islands, beating their animals
constantly, rarely resting or
watering them during the day,
and deliberately running into
people who prefer to walk up.
Most ferries now put into
another port, Athinios, which is
linked to Thira by bus.

◆◆◆
AKROTIRI

On the road from Thira to the
interesting archaeological site at
Akrotiri are hotels and pensions,
notably at Karterados, 1¼ miles
(2km) from Thira, served by a
good bus service, and at
Mesaria, 3¾ miles (6km) from
Thira. Roads lead to a volcanic-
dust beach at Monolithos,
where there are two tavernas
and a canning factory, and to
the port-resort of Kamari.
Excavations at Akrotiri, 8½ miles
(14km) from Thira, were started
in 1967 by a Greek, Professor
Marinatos. He died in 1974 and
is buried here. For a good study
of the site, read the book by his
son Dr Manos Marinatos, *Art
and Religion in Thera –
Reconstructing a Bronze Age
Society*. Thera is the name most
used by the Greeks for Santorini.
A Minoan town from around
1600BC has been unearthed. It is
not quite so impressive as
Knossos on Crete, but has
buildings up to three storeys
high, even doors, window frames
and water systems, preserved
under the lava. It is of the same
period as Knossos and proves
the close connection with Crete,
128 miles (205km) away. The
frescos discovered at Akrotiri,
including a springtime scene of
birds and flowers covering

*Santorini's black beaches (this is
Kamari), caused by volcanic activity,
do not put sun-worshippers off*

three walls, are, alas, in Athens
– 'for safe keeping'. The site's
roofing can make it very hot at
mid-day. It shuts about 15.00hrs
and closes on Mondays. Below
is a bay of pebbles and rock
with a good hotel (the Akrotiri,
tel: (0286) 81375), and a taverna
and village above with bars and
rooms among vineyards.

remains of ancient Thera, which you reach by tackling a mountain path from either side. The ruins were excavated from 1867 and date mostly from 300–145BC, when the Egyptians had a naval base at Kamari, though there was a city here 600 years earlier; erotic carvings on rocks date from the 7th century BC. Remains include temples to the Egyptian gods Isis, Seraphis and Anubis, to Dionysus, god of wine, Apollo and the Egyptian Ptolemies; a theatre with a frightening sheer drop to the sea; and inscriptions from around 800BC, recording names of participants at the gymnopaidia when young soldiers took part in athletic contests and nude dancing.

◆
KAMARI (KAMARION)
Kamari, until recently a charming fishing village with a big 'black' beach and a few hotels and tavernas, has grown into a lively resort devoted mostly to young holiday-makers, with music bars with names like Banana Moon, dancing until dawn in nightspots, waterskiing, pedaloes and surfing from the beach.
A stiff mountain path from here leads to the 17th-century monastery of Profitis Ilias at 1,857ft (566m). It has a museum of ikons, paintings and relics.

◆
PERISSA
A road across the isle leads to Perissa (9¼ miles (15km) from Thira; bus), with a black sandy beach, small hotels, rooms and tavernas. The big modern church is on the site of the Byzantine church to St Irene, from whom the name Santorini came. The mountainous headland dividing Perissa from the beach resort of Kamari (6 miles (10km) from Thira; bus), has the

◆
ATHINIOS
Now the main ferry port, 7½ miles (12km) south of Thira on the west coast, this has sands, café bars and little else. No doubt it will grow. Swarms of hotel buses meet ferries.

CYCLADES

Artefacts from the substantial Minoan town which has been excavated at Akrotiri, Santorini

OIA

The third port, Oia (Ia), 6¾ miles (11km) north of Thira, was half ruined by the last earthquake and houses still list drunkenly on the slopes. It has many churches, some rooms and simple hotels, and pumice stones on the shore which tourists collect for souvenirs. Oia is the port for excursion boats to nearby Thirasia island.

Accommodation

Thira: **Atlantis**, A-class, spectacular views, pricey (tel: (0286) 22232). **Panorama**, 1¼ miles (2km) north of town, C-class, superb views (tel: (0286) 22481). **Tataki**, in a lane from Plateia Theokopoulou (bus square) past Pelikan Tours, has rooms with showers and is good for D-class (tel: (0286) 22389). Karterados (1¼ miles (2km) from Thira): **Cyclades**, D-class, rooms with WC, shower (tel: (0286) 22948).

Messaria: **Loizos**, C-class, all rooms have WC, shower (tel: (0286) 31733). Kamari: all grades of hotels. Oia: **Fregata**, better than most D-class and dearer (tel: (0286) 71221).

Restaurants

The isle is proud of its wine. Nichteri is white and dry, Vinsanto white, sweet and strong. There is plenty of choice of eating places in Thira. Prices are rather high but meals are good. **Castro**, near the cable car, is good and pricey. **Nicholas Taverna** (just down the port steps) is cheap and may have a queue. In Oia, **George's** is good value. Kamari has many tavernas.

General information

Population 7,000
Area 37 sq miles (96 sq km)
127 nautical miles from Piraeus.
No tourist police.
Town Police: (tel: (0286) 22649).
Harbour Police: Odhos 25
March, Thira (tel: (0286) 22239).

How to get there

Air: International charters and package tours fly direct. There are flights from Athens 2 or 3 times a day in summer (55mins), from Mykonos daily (40mins), from Crete 4 times a week (40mins) and from Rhodes three times a week (1hr).
Ferries: From Piraeus (12hrs) daily, often twice a day in summer. Daily (often two boats) to Ios, Paros and Naxos; Crete 5 days a week; Mykonos 4 days a week; 2 days a week to Sikinos, Syros and Folegandros. Twice a week to Siphnos and Seriphos. Once a week to Tinos, Kimolos, Milos and Kythnos.

IONIAN ISLES

ZAKYNTHOS (ZAKINTHOS) ✓

Despite the earthquake of 1953 which destroyed most of its Venetian buildings, and a new airfield which brings a minor but growing invasion of package tourists, Zakynthos still keeps its magic.

Most package tour visitors stay either in Laganas, Argasi, or Alikes in the north, where there are a few small hotels, rooms to rent and restaurants. All these have some seasonal nightlife. The capital port, Zakynthos Town, is happy and quite lively. The rest of the island is relaxed and sleepy, with little isolated, deserted beaches and hamlets where goats, sheep, olive trees and vines take precedence over visitors. Roads are reasonably paved for exploring much of the island, but take to the other 'roads' which are really dirt mule tracks, especially in the hilly north of the isle, and life slips back two centuries. A hire car is very rewarding but a little courage is needed to tackle some roads. Wells and springs have made valleys fertile and green.

Provided that there is reasonable soil and a regular supply of water, more or less anything will grow in the sheltered valleys of Zakynthos

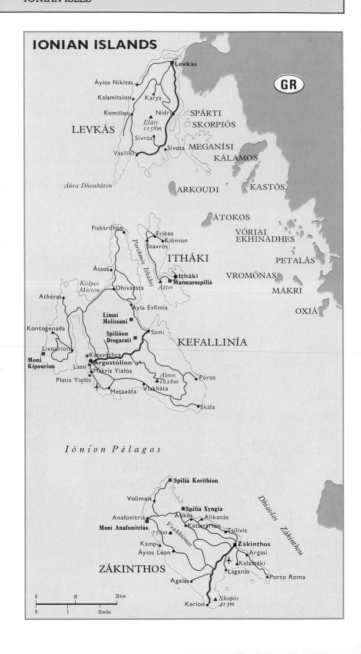

IONIAN ISLANDS

◆◆
ZAKYNTHOS (ZAKINTHOS) TOWN

Rebuilt after the earthquake in its Venetian pattern, with arcades, squares, narrow streets and little palazzi, the town is in a lively position among hills. The elegant rebuilt main square, Plateia Solomou, is named after the poet Dionysos Solomos, who died in 1857. He wrote the Greek national anthem, Hymn of Liberty, translated into English by Rudyard Kipling. Like Corfu, Zakynthos was governed by the English from 1809 to 1864. The lovely 15th-century Aghios Nikolaos Church in the corner of the square is one of the few that could be restored after the earthquake.

Fine ikons (15th–19th century) saved from wrecked churches are in the Art Museum on the square, with religious paintings of the Ionian School by artists who fled from the Turks in Crete (08.30–15.00hrs; closed Mondays). Kastro, the hillside Venetian castle, also survived the earthquake. You have a good view of town, bay and mainland coast from up there, but it can be windy (08.30–14.30hrs; closed Mondays). Zakynthos is a busy little commercial port, with cargo ships and ferries docking beside a harbour pier or right on the portside, which is lined with cafés, tavernas and souvenir shops specialising in woollen sweaters, local nougat, perfumes and liqueurs. Fishing boats land their catch, too. At the opposite end from the ferry quay is the most impressive

Zakynthos Town has a clear indigenous life of its own, quite separate from the demands of tourism

church, the rebuilt St Dionyssios, named after the island's patron. With its red roof and square white bell tower, it looks as pretty in daytime against the blue summer sky as it does lit at night and shining in the water. The inside, lit by chandeliers, is blue and white with ornate many-coloured frescos on its curved ceiling. The roads behind the harbour are narrow and packed with typically Greek-island shops in apparent disorder, cafés, restaurants, a few hotels and the bus station with fairly good services to several parts of the island. Restaurants and night life are centred around Aghios Marko square.

◆◆
LAGANAS

Laganas lures Greeks from the Peloponnese mainland as well as foreigners, so parts of its 5½ miles (9km) of soft, gently-shelving sand can still look well-populated in summer. Cars are allowed to drive on some stretches to reach hotels and apartments. It has a good choice of tavernas beside the beach and bars, tavernas and restaurants on the main road. Watersports are available, there is a disco, an open air cinema and a regular bus service into the town. It is a good place for families or lively young people, and is to be found 4½ miles (7km) south of the port.

◆◆
ARGASI

A developing village, but more relaxed than Laganas and set in more attractive scenery. Its

Summer sunset across Defni Bay, Zakynthos

sand and pebble beach is narrow but the bay is attractive, with translucent, clean water and a sandy seabed. There are several shops, some good tavernas and restaurants, bars with music nightly and discos which come and go each season. One is in an old Venetian mansion. The main road can be quite busy in summer but it is a relaxed place, with watersports. Behind is Mount Skopos which men would climb in old times to watch for pirate ships. Argasi is 2½ miles (4km) from Zakynthos.

◆
KALAMAKI

Over the mountain, 3 miles (5km) from Zakynthos, is Kalamaki, a typically Greek village with a long, wide sandy beach just starting to be developed. There are new studios, a couple of hotels, bars, a restaurant and a disco. The hilly road from Argasi leads

to attractive beaches with simple tavernas – St Nicholas and delightful Porto Roma, with a fine sweep of sand in a wooded bay. The road becomes a driveable track leading to the clean, golden sands of Vasilikos beach. Part of this is rightly closed to people, for there are more important visitors. For millions of years loggerhead turtles, endangered giants, have come in at night to lay their eggs. So please keep away.

◆
TSILIVIS
Northward from Zakynthos Town is a lush, fertile plain of orange and olive groves, and vines producing grapes for the famous Zante currants, known to Elizabethans in England. In the spring, wild flowers are lovely here. Three miles (5km) from Zakynthos Town is the farming village of Tsilivis, where olive trees meet a beach of sand as fine as talcum powder. There are two small hotels, tavernas, holiday villas and a pub.

◆◆
ALIKES
Alikes bay has a superb stretch of sand backed by dunes and salt lagoons, with lovely country behind rising to the mountains. The little resort of Alikes at the eastern end is uncommercialised, though it has the usual tavernas, tourist shops, bars and even a small roller-skating rink. There are watersports. Alikanas, a mile away, is even smaller.

SIGHTS
At the northern tip of the island are Kianoun Caves (Spiliá Korithion), known as the Blue Grotto caves. Go in the afternoon when the sun shining on the azure sea makes patterns in shades of blue on the cave walls and rock arches. In summer, caique trips go to the caves from Alikes, or you can reach them by taking a road to the sea at Volime. Here there are two tavernas, sands which get very hot and a quay where small boats sail to the caves. Further south is a big sandy bay called Smugglers' Cove (Spiliá Xyngia) visited usually by boat from Alikes, half way round the island, for there is no road to it. The wreck of a large ship rusts in the sands – rumoured to be the debris of a fortuitous insurance coup.The main road from Zakynthos Town, bypassing Laganas, reaches the natural pitch-wells of Keri, used from ancient times until recently for caulking boats and mentioned by both Pliny and Herodotus. At Keri village are fine views, and the beach below has two tavernas.
The 15th-century Monastery of Anafonitrias (Moní Anafonítrias) is 5 miles (8km) from Katastari, a town inland from Alikes. It withstood the earthquake and is kept by a few nuns who will show you the frescos, medieval tower and cell of Dionysos, patron saint of Zakynthos.
On the west side, downhill from Aghios Leontas, is the quiet village of Kampi. A track winds uphill to a sadly dramatic scene. Below a sheer clifftop is a tiny bay with near-violet seas lapping grey rocks. On a peak behind is a massive concrete cross. It is a memorial to Greek

freedom fighters who were thrown over the cliff in World War II. Incongruously there is a small modern bar-taverna here.

Festivals
Carnival is held two weeks before Lent, with masked singers and dancing. 24 August is the festival of St Dionysios.

Accommodation
The best hotel in Zakynthos Town is **Strada Marina**, 14 K Lomvardou Street, on the quay with sea and harbour views (tel: (0695) 22761/3), B-class. **Xenia**, 66 Dionissiou Roma (tel: (0695) 22232/22666), also B-class, is hidden in a narrow street. A reliable C-class hotel is in the same block as Strada Marina: **Aegli**, 12 Lomvardou Street (tel: (0695) 28317). The **Libro d'Oro**, 92 Kryoneriou Street, C-class, on the waterfront, is good value (tel: (0695) 23785). Alikes: The **Asteria** (tel: (0695) 83203) C-class is comfortable and right beside the beach. Argasi: The A-class **Akti Zakantha** (tel: (0695) 26441/3) is modern with seaview balconies. **Chryssi Akti** (tel: (0695) 28679) overlooks the beach, with terrace and balconies. **Argassi Beach Hotel** (tel: (0695) 28554), also right on the beach has a pleasant bar (C-class). The **Mimoza Beach** (tel: (0695) 22588) has bedrooms in chalets and a good restaurant overlooking the sea. Laganas: a big choice of hotels and pensions. Kalamaki: **Crystal Beach** (tel: (0695) 22917), C-class, is family-run, friendly, in good surroundings beside a beach. Tsilivis: **Hotel Tsilivi** (tel: (0695) 23109) is box-like and small, but friendly.

The path to the beach from the White Rocks Hotel, Cephalonia

Restaurants
Zakynthos produces a good local white wine, Verdea, as well as a local brandy, ouzo and strawberry liqueur. Meals are well above average, especially in beach resorts and Zakynthos Town, though among the restaurants around Aghios Marko square and the town hall are some pizza and Greek fast food establishments.

In Zakynthos Town dine with a view at **Alla**, Filikon 38, in an old house. Eat well at **Petas Evangelos**, Alex Roma Street, where food is freshly prepared and the service enthusiastic.

General information

Population 32,000
Area 161 sq miles (417 sq km)
Tourist Office & Tourist Police:
at town hall (tel: (0695) 22200).
Harbour Police: (tel: (0695)
22417).

How to get there

Air: From Athens (2–6 flights
daily); from Cephalonia (2-3
weekly). Charter flights from
many European countries from
mid-April to mid-October.
Ferries. 3 daily (6–9 in summer)
to Kyllini on the Peloponnese
coast (1¼hrs). Some boats go in
summer to Argostoli on
Cephalonia; speed boats go to
Patras in summer.
Coach: Athens via Kyllini (7hrs).

CEPHALONIA (KEFALLINIA) ✓

Cephalonia (or Kefalonia) has
been described as an island of
dramatic mountainous beauty
and ugly prefabricated buildings.
Nature is responsible for both.
It suffered even more than
Zakynthos from the 1953
earthquake, so few remains are
left of its Mycenaean and
Classical past, or of its Venetian
heritage of fine buildings. It
lives by trade, shipping and
agriculture, not tourism, so that
its capital and main port,
Argostoli, has been rebuilt as a
working city, not for the
convenience or delight of
tourists. The town's beaches
and coves and most tourist hotels
are a 1¾ mile (3km) bus ride
away. But the centre and north
of the island have awesome
mountain drives with good views.

◆◆
ARGOSTOLI (ARGOSTOLION)

Argostoli is busy with a big
market, shops, bars, cafés and
restaurants, providing for locals
rather than visitors, around the
attractive modern Ioannou
Metaxa Square. Metaxa was a
local man: dictator of Greece in
1940, he defied the Italian
dictator Mussolini and became
a Greek hero.
Argostoli was famous pre-1953
for its bell towers, and a few
have been rebuilt, notably the
German-style tower of the
Catholic church near the square.
When the British administered
these isles, they built the
Drapanos bridge across the
narrow gulf, with low arches,
leaving a good fishing lagoon. It

leads to the little Lassi peninsula and the geological oddity called Katavothri (swallow holes), where the sea is sucked into two large tunnels under the ground. They were long used for driving sea mills. Since the earthquake they have become a trickle. No-one knew where the water went until 1963, when a geologist poured in a lot of dye. Fifteen days later it appeared in the lake of Melisani cave and near Sami, right across the island. Across Lassi peninsula above the lagoon are the high walls of the 7th-century BC acropolis of Krani. The best organised beaches are at Lassi, and also 2-3 miles (3-5 km) south of Argostoli (Makris Yalos and Platis Yalos), on the airport road. Buses run regularly from mid-June to mid-September. Bus services are reasonable on Cephalonia; in summer, taxis are numerous and boats go to popular beaches.

◆◆
LIXOURION

A car ferry goes 12 times a day (8 on Sundays) from Argostoli to the quiet little port of Lixourion across the gulf (½hr, or 20 miles round by road). Rebuilt, with wide streets, it is a pleasant town divided by a river and centred round a little square. It has its own fishing boats, so its tavernas serve good fish. (Try Anthony's, by the ferry: good food and he speaks English well.) Beaches are along the coast southwards, mostly in little sandy coves. Across the peninsula is Kipoureon (Moní Kipouríon) monastery, in its lovely setting with guest cells.

◆◆
POROS

Ferries from Kyllini on the Peloponnese mainland go either to Argostoli (2¾hrs) or Poros (Porou) (1½hrs), a little east-coast port growing into a resort. The road from Argostoli to Poros, 28 miles (45km) along the south coast is not so dramatic as those northwards, but has slopes thick with olives and cypresses and sea views. You pass through neat modern-looking villages rebuilt after the earthquake. At one of these, Metaxata, Byron wrote much of his satirical poem *Don Juan*. Poros is still being rebuilt after the earthquake damage and is not pretty but friendly, with genuine tavernas, a few small hotels and a long shingle beach with clear aquamarine seas. The countryside is rich in spring with wild flowers, lemon trees and olives. The big restaurant of the Hotel Hercules has a terrace and dining room overlooking the bay from a rock. There are little restaurants in the harbour and tavernas over the hill beside the beach. There is a small disco, but 'nightlife' is really confined to eating, drinking and chatting. Almost everything shuts down off season.

◆
SCALA (SKALA)

Five miles (8km) south of Poros is the village of Scala with a stretch of golden sand enormous by Greek standards, almost undeveloped but with a few tavernas, a store and two bars. A few villas let rooms, so does the Miabeli taverna.

◆
SAMI

The road from Argostoli to Sami,
another small port on the east
coast, is truly dramatic, climbing
through the mountains past
Mount Ainos (5,312ft, 1,619m).
On fine days there are views to
Zakynthos, Kyllini's Venetian
castle, mainland mountains and
the isles of Ithaca and Lefkas. An
energetic walk to a hut at 3,937ft
(1,200m) leads on through the
historic Cephalonian firs to
Megalos Soros, another 985ft
(300m) up.

Sami (the ancient capital Same
of Homer's days, 15½ miles
(25km) from Argostoli) was
devastated by the earthquake
and much of it is still
prefabricated. The bay is
attractive. It is the port for Ithaca
ferries and has a daily ferry
from mainland Patras (4hrs)
which itself is linked to Venice,
Ancona and Brindisi.

◆◆◆
CAVES

Near to Sami are several
strange caves. Spiliáon
Drogarati has impressively-lit,
many-coloured stalactites and
stalagmites and its acoustics are
so good that concerts are held
in it.

Limni Melissani ('Purple Cave')
a mile (2km) north on the road
towards the charming fishing
port of Aghias Evfimia, has a
deep circular bowl 250ft round,
with a lake at the bottom which
changes colour from blue to
purple with changing light.
Once it was believed to be
bottomless and unreachable. An
underground cavern known to
the ancient Greeks was found in
the 1960s and opened up as a
route to the lake. With a guide
you can take a boat on it.

*The attractive port of Sami is used
by ferries as well as fishing boats*

There is a breath-taking view from the top of the hillside overlooking Assos Bay

♦♦♦
NORTHERN CEPHALONIA (KEFALLINIA)

For the superb climbing drive northwards from Argostoli it is worth hiring a taxi for the day. At the pretty village of Divarata there is a hair-raising drive down a track to the beach, but there is a lovely view down there and another dazzling view as the road meets the coast. Look down the cliffs to the beach and blue sea of Myrtos Bay. The mountain scenery becomes more dramatic towards the little fishing town of Assos, 18½ miles (30km) from Argostoli, where there is the most beautiful scene of all. From the white quayside, red-roofed white houses spread up a hillside and onto a strip of land cutting into the sea to join a tiny peninsula – a rugged hill, terraced fields and olive groves capped by a 16th-century Venetian fortress, built as defence against Turkish pirates. The views are beautiful.

North from Assos round the north tip of the isle you pass woods of cypresses and deserted bays to reach the fishing village of Fiscardon. Little touched by the earthquake, it shows you what Cephalonia was like before the 1953 disaster and is the most delightful place on the island. Ask about rooms to rent at the village shop on the tiny square where buses arrive, or at the quayside Captain's Cabin taverna, where the owner and his wife speak English. You will get good fish in the Thendrinos restaurant and the Nicholas taverna, and lobster at a price at Hirodotos taverna. Fiscardon *is* a bit pricey.

Festivals

Carnival is held at Argostoli on the last Sunday and Monday before Lent. 15 May is the Festival of the Radicals (celebrating union with Greece) in Argostoli.

Accommodation

Cephalonia Star Hotel, 50 Metaxa Street, almost opposite the ferry, is convenient (tel: (0671) 23180/3). Also C-class, **Aegli**, 21st Maiou Street (street joining square to waterfront) is cheap but has a shared bathroom (tel: (0671) 22522).

The best hotels are found at the beaches. Lassi: **Mediterranée**, A-grade, on its private beach, informal; all rooms with private WC and shower; seawater pool; restaurant, soundproofed disco – a good family hotel (tel: (0671) 28761/3). Platis Yialos: **White Rocks**, A-class hotel-bungalow complex, air-conditioning (tel: (0671) 28332/4). Sami: **Ionion**, 5 Horofylakis, near ferry (tel: (0674) 22035). Platia Kyprou: **Kyma** (in the main square), D-grade and simple (tel: (0674) 22064). Poros: **Hercules Hotel**, B-class pension (tel: (0674) 72351), on rocks between the ferry harbour and town square, small pebble beach. **Hotel Kefalos**, in town square, all rooms with WC, shower, balcony (tel: (0674) 72139-41). Fiscardon: **Panormos Pension**, B-class; book ahead (tel: (0674) 51340). Lixourion: **Hotel Summery**, C-grade; best in town (tel: (0671) 91771).

Restaurants

Robola, made on the island, is one of the best white wines in Greece. In Argostoli the **Argostoli** restaurant next to the Rex cinema serves good cheap Greek food. **Taverna Demosthenes** just off the square is friendly, serves good fresh dishes. **Kefalos** restaurant on left side of the square is recommended for cheap meals; **Kanaria**, top left of the square, for good slightly dearer meals. The **Port of Cephalos** along the waterfront serves the best food and is 'fashionable'.

General information

Population 28,000
Area 301½ sq miles (781 sq km)

Tourist Office: (tel: (0671) 22248).
Tourist Police: Cruise liner quay (tel: (0671) 22200).
Harbour Police: (tel: (0671) 22224).

How to get there

Air: There are flights daily from Athens; from Zakynthos 2–3 times a week. Some charters fly direct from other European countries.
Ferries: from Kyllini (Peloponnese) 2 daily to Poros (1½hrs) or Argostoli (2¾hrs). Some boats go to Zakynthos in summer. From Sami to Patras (mainland) daily in summer; Sami to Ithaca daily (1hr); from Sami or Fiscardon to Corfu (one a week from each). In summer a caique goes from Fiscardon to the isle of Lefkas (50mins).
Coach: From Athens via Patras.

ITHACA (ITHAKI)

Only a rocky 17 miles long and 4 miles wide (27 x 6.5km), Ithaca is famous as the home of Odysseus, hero of Homer's *Odyssey*. A simple place with friendly people, it attracts few tourists although it is only 1¼ miles (2km) from Cephalonia at its nearest point and now has a modern road almost from top to bottom and another round much of the coast. Most visitors come for the day and are gone by 18.00hrs, but yachts stay longer.

◆◆
VATHI (ITHAKI TOWN)

Vathi, port and capital, was where Odysseus was dumped, to sleep after his 20 years' adventurous journey from the Siege of Troy. It is hidden in a deep long inlet like a fjord, past a high headland, and is almost surrounded by green conical hills. Houses joined by steep steps cling to the slopes. There is a small archaeological museum.

The isle is shaped like two bulges joined by a narrow strip ½ mile wide. At this narrow point is Mount Aetos (Eagle), where eagles still nest.

A ½ hour walk west of Vathi takes you to the Cave of the Nymphs (Marmarospiliá), which Odysseus visited incognito immediately on his return, to hide gifts brought from Corfu. Surrounded by cypress trees, the cave has a narrow entrance to a 50ft (15m) chamber, with a hole in the roof cut to let out the smoke of sacrificial fires, called 'The Entrance of the Gods'. The caves are open in high summer. Otherwise apply at Vathi town hall for the keys.

A rewarding signposted walk of 3 miles (5km) south from Vathi, past a clifftop, leads to Arethusa's fountain. Poor Arethusa cried so much when her son died that she turned into a fountain. Homer's story says that here Odysseus was recognised by his old dog, though he had been away 20 years.

STAVROS

Odysseus's city is now said to be in the north at Stavros, 10½ miles (17km) from Vathi. It is little more than a street and a square, half-filled with the chairs and tables of a real, simple taverna. Nearby at Polis Bay is a quay used by fishing boats, and from here some tourist boats go to Fiscardon on Cephalonia.

FRIKES

The charming fishing village of Frikes runs along an attractive valley to a little square and port, with a hotel and tavernas. There is a sailing centre, and boats go to Vathi and also, if you are lucky, to Vassiliki on Lefkas. On a hillside 2½ miles (4km) away, overlooking its port, is the prettiest village on Ithaca, Kioni. There are food shops, several tavernas and very small beaches. A good hideaway, Frikes is 12½ miles (20km) across the island from Vathi.

Accommodation

The best and most modern hotel in Vathi is the **Mendor** (B-grade), Georg Drakouli Street, out of town centre, open only in summer (tel: (0674) 32433). Cheaper, simpler but more convenient is **Aktaeon**, near the ferry-boat quay: E-grade, English spoken (tel: (0674) 32387).

Restaurants

The main square of Vathi has a row of pavement taverna-cafés. The best is **Penelope**, with a downstairs bar and upstairs restaurant offering varied dishes. Best food in town is at a taverna called simply **Taverna**, offering charcoal-grilled meat, fish and souvlaki, and pots of Greek dishes simmering on the stove. You can tell it is good, because it is a meeting place for locals. It is behind the town hall opposite the popular **Pension Enoikiazomena** (old rooms; cheap).

General information

Population 3,600
Area 37 sq miles (96 sq km)
Tourist Office & Tourist Police:
in police station (tel: (0674)
32205).
Harbour Police: (tel: (0674)
31206). House on jetty: (tel:
(0674) 32909).
Buses are scarce. Roads can be
rough for scooters. Taxis
reasonably priced.

How to get there

Ferries: daily from Vathi to Sami
on Cephalonia (1hr) and on to
Patras (mainland, 5hrs). Every
other day to Paxos and Corfu.
Daily to Astakos on the
mainland (1¾hrs). In summer
there are boats from Stavros to
Fiscardon (Cephalonia) and
from Frikes to Vassiliki (Lefkas).
Coach: From Athens via Patras.

LEFKAS (LEVKAS)

The bus direct from Athens
does not have to board a ferry
to reach Lefkas (or Lefkada), for
the isle is joined to the province
of Aetolia-Akarnania on the
mainland by a causeway with a
wide road. It became an island
in 540BC when Corinthian
colonists cut a canal, which was
widened by the Venetians. You
can also cross by a chain-ferry.

◆◆
LEFKAS (LEVKAS) TOWN

Lefkas suffered from an
earthquake in 1948 when
Greece was too poor for much
rebuilding. So some upper
storeys of buildings are still of
boarding and corrugated iron.
But there are old stone
churches with solid bell towers
and tall houses with Turkish
wooden balconies and with
flowers and plants as covering,
so there is no hint of shanty-
town. The big quay is a yacht-
chartering centre. There is the
usual archaeological museum,
an Ikon Museum in the public
library, a Folklore museum and
the Lefkada Sound Museum (29
Kalkari Street) founded by a
local collector with old
gramophones sent over by

*Lefkas is a quiet little place, with an
abundance of good produce*

relatives from the US, records of Greek songs from the 1920s and some 1914 recordings. The east coast is dotted with pleasant villages. Vliho, in a fjord-like bay lined with mountains, is delightfully quiet. Nidri is a lovely fishing port with fine views of a bay with tiny islands. Sailing flotillas call. There are rooms to let in villas and tavernas. Ferries go from Nidri to the little green isle of Meganisi (tranquil, with some rooms in the three villages). South from Nidri is a delightful little fishing port, Syvoto, with grass to the water's edge. Buses go twice a day from Lefkas Town to Kalamisti on the west coast, which has the best beach, but you must tackle a steep track of hairpin bends, potholes and boulders to reach the sea.

VASSILIKI (VASILIKI)

Buses serve several towns and villages but only twice a day, except to Nidri and the equally attractive fishing village of Vassiliki. It is on the south coast about 24 miles (38km) from Lefkas. There is a board sailing school in Vassiliki at Hotel Lefkatas. From here caiques sail to several nearby islands, including Cephalonia. From Vassiliki you can go by caique or by road (rough) via Komili to Cape Doukato – the original Lover's Leap. From here Sappho, poetess of love from Lesbos, leapt to her death, dying for love of a handsome boatman. The priests from Apollo's temple made the jump successfully as part of their ritual. Rumour has it that they used a net.

Festivals
International Folklore Festival, last two weeks of August.

Accommodation
Behind the main quay of Lefkas port are three B-class, fairly good hotels, with bedrooms with WC and shower: **Xenia Lefkas**, overlooking canal (tel: (0645) 24762/3); **Niricos**, Paralia (tel: (0645) 24132); **Lefkas**, 2 Panagou Street (tel: (0645) 23916/8). Others include **Santa Mavra** in the small square, Odhos Darfeld, off the High Street behind the lagoon, C-class (tel: (0645) 22342)

Restaurants
Lefkas specialises in salads made with fried marinated fish. Prices rise in places where flotilla yachts call. Lefkas Town: **Lighthouse** taverna (in alley opposite the church) has excellent food. Other good tavernas are **Romantica** (Ioan Mala – main street) and **Pete's** (on the square behind the lagoon). Vassiliki: **Taverna Ionian** opposite Post Office (simple, cheap). Nidri: good tavernas along the waterfront.

General information
Population 24,000
Area 114 sq miles (295 sq km).
Tourist Police: (tel: (0645) 22346).

How to get there
Air: Flights to Aktion from Athens, plus summer charters.
Ferries: Chain-ferry from Preveza to Aktion beside causeway. Summer caiques go from Vassiliki to Vathi (Ithaca) and Fiscardon (Cephalonia).
Coaches: Athens–Aktion, then across the causeway (7hrs).

DODECANESE
KARPATHOS (CARPATHOS)

Karpathos changes more slowly than any other of the 12 Dodecanese Islands. There are not enough roads or rooms to lure many tourists, and only a few buses, running in summer; use taxis. Not until 1979 was there a road linking the fertile south and the mountainous north, and many people still go between them by boat. Now, as well as an air link with Rhodes and Crete with very small planes (15-seaters), a few charter planes land from Britain. Most visitors are emigrants from the US returning to see families or to find an island girl to marry. The Pan Karpathian Society of America symbolises a tight community keeping alive the island's culture, publishing a magazine and even choosing an annual 'Miss Karpathos'.

The island is quite rich, exporting citrus fruit and vegetables, and is said to have the highest income of any Greek Isle from emigrants working abroad. Some men need to emigrate because of a tradition that family inheritance goes not to the eldest son but the eldest daughter. A compelling reason for emigration in the old days was foreign occupation! The Dodecanese, including Rhodes, were not freed from the Turks until 1912.

◆◆
PIGADIA (KARPATHOS TOWN)

Ferries call at the thriving little port of Pigadia, or Karpathos, in the south and Diafani in the north. Pigadia, in a bay where mountains meet sea, has quite a

Vrontis Bay, Karpathos

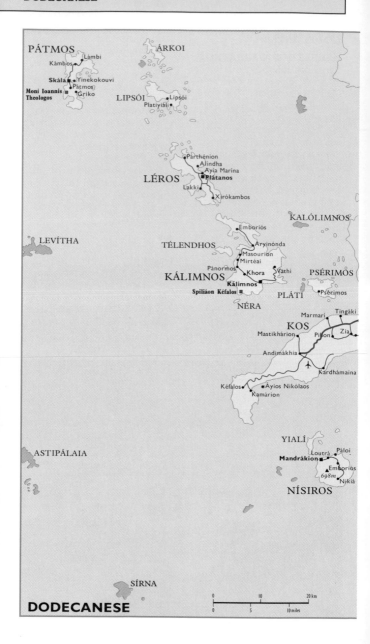

PÁTMOS
Lámbi
Kámbos
Skála
Yinekokouvi
Moni Ioannis
Theologos
Pátmos
Gríko

ÁRKOI

LIPSÓI
Lipsói
Platiyiáli

LEVÍTHA

LÉROS
Parthénion
Alindha
Ayía Marina
Plátanos
Lakki
Xirókambos

KALÓLIMNOS

TÉLENDHOS
Emboriós
Aryinónda
Masourión
Mirtéai
Pánormos
Khora
Vathi
KÁLIMNOS
Kálimnos
Spiliáon Kéfalos

PSÉRIMOS
Psérimos

PLÁTI

NÉRA

KOS
Marmari
Tingáki
Mastikhárion
Pilíon
Zía
Andimákhia
Kardhámaina
Kéfalos
Áyios Nikólaos
Kamárion

ASTIPÁLAIA

YIALÍ
Loutrá
Páloi
Mandrákion
Emboriós
698m
Nikiá
NÍSIROS

SÍRNA

DODECANESE

0   10   20 km
0   5   10 miles

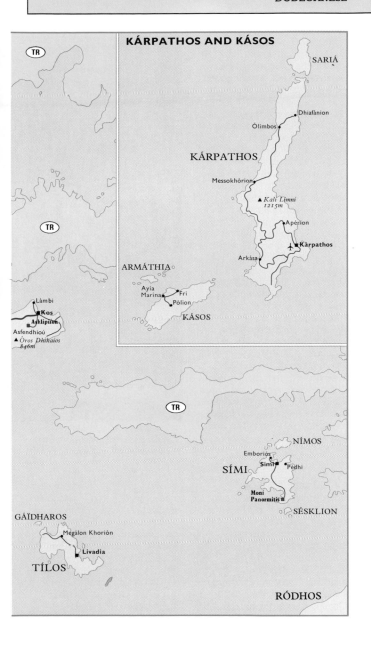

KÁRPATHOS AND KÁSOS

lot of small hotels, pensions and rooms and is building more. A road leads from here to the small beach resort of Ammopi, with a string of small beaches, tavernas and rooms.

There are several quiet beaches up the east coast, accessible by land or by boat. Apella is in a dramatic setting of rugged rock formations, steep gorges and huge boulders left by the Titans of Greek legend. These giants tore lumps off the mountain to throw at each other. Aghios Nikolaos, a fishing village further north, has a few rooms and a taverna owned by a fisherman, whose wife cooks the catch.

A road crosses the isle to Finiki (harbour of Arkassa), a large fishing village and caique port, with a very good fish taverna. Just south are relics of ancient Arkassa, on a clifftop. Some good Byzantine mosaics remain, though the Italians took most to Rhodes. A rough road up the west coast from Finiki leads to Lefkos, with a white sand beach, shading pines, a small hotel and tavernas. Boats go from Pigadia to the nearby island of Kassos (Kasos), where there are fine walks and solitude.

You have to be fit to live in – or visit – the awe-inspiring town of Olympos

OLYMPOS (OLIMBOS)

The road to Olympos in the north, 37 miles (60km) from Pigadia, is reasonable as far as Aperi, the old capital, which has a cathedral containing an ikon credited with several miracles. Then it deteriorates, but around the scary corners you see some fine sea and mountain views. Olympos is beautiful and dramatic. It is clamped to a mountain ridge,

its white, blue and beige houses, many with decorative balconies, are terraced upwards and joined by alleys and donkey steps. No car can get past the first taverna. A line of windmills runs down the edge. The mountain dives from the village to the sea on one side, steps down by cultivated terraces to a fertile valley on the other. Some believe that the people of Olympos are descended from

Dorian Greeks of 3,000 years ago. They use words, it seems, seen today only in Homer. Unmarried girls wear old gold jewellery, some made from gold foreign coins sent home by fathers working abroad. When they marry, they put the gold away to pass to their daughters. There is no bus from Pigadia to Olympos. Share a taxi, or take a boat to the northern port of Diafani, about 25 miles (40km) up the coast, and a shorter taxi or minibus ride from there on a track-road.

◆
DIAFANI (DHIAFANION)
This is a small, pleasant resort with a beach backed by pine woods, and a few rooms and tavernas. The Mayflower Hotel has six rooms and a good fish restaurant. A boat goes on Sundays to the tiny isle of Saria, deserted except for summer shepherds. A hard walk leads to Ta Palatia (the Palaces), small stone domed houses, once a pirate base.

Accommodation
Pigadia: **Porfyris**, C-class, clean, close to beach; good meals (tel: (0245) 22294).

Restaurants
Pigadia: **George's**, below the bank, has fine seafood.
Olympos: **Artemis Pension** has excellent fish dishes.

General information
Population 6,500
Area 117 sq miles (304 sq km)
227 nautical miles from Piraeus.
Tourist Police: (tel: (0245) 22218).

How to get there
Air: There are flights twice daily from Rhodes (40mins), several a week from Crete (Sitia) (45mins) and three times a week from Kassos.
Ferries: 4 times a week from Piraeus (23hrs); twice a week from Rhodes (7½hrs), Kassos, Crete and Halki.

SYMI (SIMI) ✓

Symi is so attractively serene that people on day excursions from Rhodes or Kos sometimes jump ship and stay for days. Wily visitors take the island's only bus,

DODECANESE

or walk through fields of oregano, to the pebbly beach at Pedi, which has an hotel and tavernas, and where they also repair caiques.

You sail into the harbour past steep cliffs sheer to the sea. Rounding a point you see the harbour like a fjord of deep blue, ending in the town of white and ochre houses with red roofs. Alongside the boats are neo-classical houses built last century from the profits of ship building and sponge-diving. These were empty and crumbling until recently. Now many are being restored, even to their mosaic courtyards. One on the quayside round the headland is a small, tasteful A-class hotel, the Aliki (see page 73). Symi dare not build many hotels or encourage too many visitors to stay because of a water shortage, so the tavernas at night are packed with as many locals eating, drinking and talking as visitors.

By day, the harbour quay is constantly busy, with boats landing fish, vegetables from Rhodes, and black sponges to be washed and beaten clean. Caiques come and go taking visitors to remote beaches of the island, to Nimos, the isle of shepherds to the north, where visitors can swim, fish and walk, or to fertile Sesklia southward, owned by the monks of Panormitis monastery. Boat-building made Symi prosperous. When the Knights of St John were there they let Symians go their own way so long as they built them fast solid ships. The Turks so liked the Symian skaphes, fast-sailing courier boats, that they allowed Symians to own

Symi has been known through the centuries for its caiques, boats and ships

land on the shores of Turkey, and gave them the right to dive for sponges in any Turkish-controlled waters in return for sponges for the ladies of Sultan Suleiman's harem.

Symi's depression started when the Italians took the Dodecanese in 1912 and cut off the Symians from their Turkish lands. The population dropped from 20,000 to 2,200 as the young emigrated to Rhodes, Athens, America and Australia. Tourism and fishing have restored prosperity.

The port is two towns: the harbour area, Ghialos, joined by Kali Strata, a 'high street' of 357 steps, to Chorio, the high town, 275 more steps lead to a monastery. Mules and donkeys carry most things – even building materials. It is a long way round by the bus road. You must walk or take a truck-ride into the interior and mountains where pine and cypress flourish. A road now runs to Panormitis monastery (Moní Panormitis), on a horseshoe bay 9 miles (5km) south. There are no buses, but some excursions, and excursion boats from Rhodes to Ghialos port call here. The building is mostly 18th century, with a mock baroque bell tower built in 1905. The little chapel has a remarkable carved ikon, and the museum has beautiful votive offerings of carved model ships and little bottles which passing sailors threw out to drift ashore with money for the monastery. It has a restaurant, café, food shop and cells where you can stay. You should make a donation when you leave. Symi remains very Greek despite its nearness to Turkey.

Accommodation
It is advisable to pre-book rooms in high summer. **Aliki**, A-class, is a lovely old house (tel: (0241) 71665); booking essential. **Dorian**, another old house, costs much the same (tel: (0241) 71181). **Nireus** (next door to Aliki) is modern bungalow style, B-class (tel: (0241) 71386). For monastery accommodation (200 cell-like rooms), phone (0241) 71354.

Restaurants
Shrimps and lobsters are especially good on Symi. Fragosyko, a local version of Turkish Delight made from figs, is worth trying. **Les Katerinettes** (also a pension) is one of the best places to eat near the harbour, but most tavernas are worth trying. **George's**, in the Chorio, has good views.

General information
Population 2,200
Area 20½ sq miles (53 sq km)
230 nautical miles from Piraeus.
Tourist Police: (tel: (0241) 71111).

How to get there
Ferries: From Rhodes daily in summer, fewer in winter (2hrs); 1 or 2 a week from Piraeus, Astipalaia, Amorgos, Kalymnos, Kos, Leros, Nisiros, Paros, Patmos, Samos and Tilos.

KOS
Kos has rocketed into popularity since the airfield was extended, and bids to join Corfu, Crete and Rhodes as one of the big tourist isles of Greece. It has not quite happened yet. True, the old lazy waterfront of Kos Town now seethes with people walking, cycling, or eating and

drinking at the pavement taverna tables, and with coaches, taxis and bicycles. Flotilla yachts and more luxurious craft slap against the fishing boats at the quayside. Side roads are packed with more bars and restaurants, shops selling clothes, leather goods and liquor at Kos's duty-free prices, and travel agents offering excursions to other isles. Round the harbour towards Lampi new roads are thick with new little modern hotels, small apartment blocks, shops and restaurants. The ghosts of the Knights of St John who built the formidable medieval castle at the harbour's end must look in wonder at the noisy hydrofoils making for other isles, tourists hang-gliding over the beach and girls sunbathing topless. And across the island Kardamena has developed in a few years from a fishing port with fish tavernas on its quay into a lively little resort with hotels, small apartment blocks, tavernas crowded in summer, and a beach thick with browning bodies. There are noisy water-scooters, too, and discos. But somehow it retains much of its fishing port atmosphere. And the farming villages of the interior and remoter beaches of Kos reached by mule track bear no relation to the scene in Kos Town. Kos has many good roads where scooters are safe for experienced drivers. There are fairly good bus services in summer, plenty of taxis, and cars for hire. Many visitors hire bicycles.

◆◆
KOS TOWN

The town is a jolly place, with infectious happiness and relaxation. Even its crumbling Italian mansions have a certain decadent charm. And the fishermen still sell their catch on the quay to passers-by. It is surprising how Kos has remained so Greek, despite being occupied from 197BC, when the Romans took over, until 1945 when the British Army freed it from the Germans who had taken it in 1943 from the Italians. Under Mussolini all education was in Italian and farms were given to Italian immigrants, turning local Greek farmers into farm workers.

In the town, Ancient Greek ruins are scattered around so liberally that locals treat them casually. The well-restored amphitheatre is sometimes used as an open-air theatre. The Archaeological Museum is interesting, with mosaics from the 3rd century AD and statues, including Hermes with a dog (08.30– 15.00hrs; closed Mondays). Apart from the 15th-century Knight's castle, there are interesting old Turkish mosques. But the important site is truly Greek. Hippocrates, 'Father of Modern Medicine', was born here about 460BC. He preached diagnosis by observation and treatment by baths and diet. (The priests believed in magical cures.) A huge old twisted plane tree by the castle is where he is supposed to have taught his pupils. In fact, it is a mere 600 years old.

◆◆
THE ASKLEPEION (ASKLIPIION)

Two and a half miles (4km) south of Kos is the Asklepeion, built in the 4th century BC, after Hippocrates died. It is a shrine to the healing god Asklepeios, whose priests believed that baths in a lovely setting were good for body and soul. Snakes were their symbol and have remained a medical symbol ever since. The temple drew people suffering with problems from baldness to blindness. The site is set on four levels, once graced by altars and statues, near springs with iron content – the fountain of Pan.

◆◆
LAMPI (LAMBI)
The beach north of the town has many tavernas and at Lampi, 4¼ miles (7km) north is the primitive-looking taverna Faros, which serves some of the best taverna food in the Greek Isles. Choose from raw fresh fish, meat on the slab and copper pots on the cooker. A new B-class hotel at Lampi, the little Cosmopolitan (tel: (0242) 23411/5) is very friendly.

OTHER BEACHES
A sand beach along the north coast, Tingaki (8¾ miles (14km) from Kos Town), with good fish tavernas and a number of package-tour hotels, has fine sand but winds. The fishing village of Marmari, 10 miles (16km) from Kos, has a few hotels and a nearby beach. Mastihari, a fishing village with a shaded beach 15½ miles (25km) from Kos Town, is pleasant. Boats go from here to the isles of Pserimos and Kalymnos. Kephalos, 26¾ miles (43km) from Kos, just inland from the east coast, has a ruined Knights' castle with a medieval legend of a dragon

Kos Town: the tree forming part of the background is the famous Hippocrates Tree. Kos Town is described on page 74

living in a cave, and the ruins of Astypalaia, ancient capital of the island. A beach ½ mile (1km) away at Kamari has a fishing boat quay, a taverna and a rocky islet, Aghios Nikolaos, with a fishermen's chapel. Tavernas along the bay lead to a Club Méditerranée with watersports in magnificently blue clear sea and nude sunbathing on the rocks. Then begins Paradissos Bay (Almiros) with good sands but no shade. The sea is warm and slightly bubbly from the volcanic seabed.

Kardamena up the coast and 18 miles (29km) from Kos Town, is still a superb place for tasting fish, but is not a good centre for inter-island touring. Boats and hydrofoils nearly all go from Kos Town before the buses from Kardamena arrive, so taxis are often necessary from here.

INLAND VILLAGES

Pili, 10½ miles (17km) southwest of Kos Town, is a mountain village with superb views to the sea. A 2½ mile (4km) path leads to the remains of a Byzantine castle. Asfendiou, on the slopes of Mount Dikaios, 9 miles (14km) from Kos Town, is really five hamlets. Zia is beautiful, with steep white alleys, courtyards where they bake bread, and many flowers. Excursion coaches call in during the day, and in the evening to see the sunset, watch Greek dancing and taste the wine. This is a wine district. Some renovated houses are let to visitors (ask the Tourist Office in Kos Town for bookings – (0242) 24400). May and September are good months for Kos, but then there are fewer boats to other islands.

Accommodation

Some new 'Costa' style hotels with pools and discos have been built, but you would do better to take bed and breakfast at one of the many pensions or small hotels. Most are new, clean, family run, with good plumbing. The most luxurious hotel is the **Ramira Beach** outside Kos Town in Psalidi, A-class (tel: (0242) 22891/4). **Astron**, near the harbour (B-class), is modern, with good views from the

rooftop garden (tel: (0242) 23705/7). Kardamena: **Norida Beach** complex is 'international'; A-class (tel: (0242) 91231/2). **Stelios** on the main square is more fun, but book ahead (tel: (0242) 91293). Between Kardamena and Kephalos, is the A-class **Lakitira** (tel: (0242) 91115).

Restaurants

Eat in very Greek tavernas, as some restaurants serve bland 'international' food. Tavernas in Kos Town are mostly popular and a little pricey. **Limani** on the waterfront is fashionable and offers good Greek food. The **Bristol Taverna's Garden** restaurant is popular and the Bristol hotel is a small clean bed and breakfast pension (tel: (0242) 22865).

General information

Population 21,350
Area 112 sq miles (290 sq km)
192 nautical miles from Piraeus.
Tourist Office: (tel: (0242) 24400).
Tourist Police: next door to Tourist Office (tel: (0242) 24444).
Harbour Police: (tel: (0242) 28527).

How to get there

Air: There are charters from several European capitals. Flights from Athens arrive 1–3 times a day, from Rhodes most days, and from Mykonos four times a week in July and August. **Ferries**: daily from Piraeus (14hrs), Patmos, Leros, Kalymnos and Rhodes; 2–3 a week from Nissyros, Tilos and Symi. There are irregular services to Chios, Lesbos, Lemnos, Crete, Santorini and Milos, and dozens of excursions

A general view of the little port of Myrties, across Kalymnos

in summer.

Hydrofoils: irregular service June–September from Rhodes, Patmos, Samos and Leros.

KALYMNOS (KALIMNOS)

Kalymnos' port is frantic, noisy and great fun. Its wealth still comes from sponge-diving. Sponges of all shapes, sizes and quality hang on strings from shops and stalls, and this is what lures so many day-trippers from Rhodes and Kos. Usually they make straight for the sponge factory to see how the sponges, black when they arrive, are washed, dried and treated with acid to turn them a pleasant yellow. At Easter, the isle celebrates for a week with music, dancing in local costume, eating and free drinks before the sponge boats leave to the peal of church bells. They return with

their sponges in October to another round of celebrations. Diving is not so dangerous as in the days when divers strapped heavy stones to their chests to reach the sea bed. Now they wear oxygen tanks and attack sponges with axes. It is doubtful if the business can last much longer. The divers face tough competition from Cubans who dive in rich sponge fields off the Florida Keys and undercut Greek prices, even offering sponges to shops on Kalymnos to sell to tourists. Ironically it was Kalymniot divers who started the business in Florida.

◆◆
POTHIA (KALIMNOS TOWN)

Pothia harbour is packed with ships, and hotels and tavernas stretch round the harbour bay to the little beach. In this scrum are some fine works of art. Aghia Ekaterini Church on the harbour has beautiful decorations in gold, blue and brown, and superb ikons by famous local artists. Local sculptors Michail Kokkinos and his daughter Irene have adorned the town with statues. Two works are *Winged Victory* in Liberty Square, and *Poseidon* by the Olympic Hotel.

The island, which looks barren and rocky as you approach, has hidden fertile valleys of figs, mandarins, lemons and vines. One valley with three villages growing lemons, oranges, mandarins and roses leads to the delightful fishing hamlet of Vathi, with its tiny harbour and two tavernas at the end of a long fjord, 7½ miles (12km) from Pothia. Buses are infrequent, it is best to share taxis on Kalymnos.

BEACHES

Across the island are the sandy beaches: Panormos, Myrties, from where boats go to Telendos, Massouri and Emborios. The north is deserted.

◆◆◆
LEROS

Prosperous, off the beaten track and not beautiful, Leros (20½ sq miles, 53 sq km) has little foreign tourism. Mussolini made Leros a hospital isle for the mentally sick. There are still 3 hospitals, employing a quarter of its population of 8,000.

Accommodation

Myrties: **Themis** has sea views over Telendos whose sunsets are famous, B-class (tel: (0243) 47230). The **Myrties Hotel** is D-class (tel: (0243) 28912).

Restaurants

Tavernas are mostly by the beaches and around Pothia harbour. **Stelios Restaurant** is still the most popular in Pothia.

In Myrties, the **Myrties** has a veranda with harbour views.

General information

Population 14,300
Area 43 sq miles (111 sq km)
183 nautical miles from Piraeus.
Tourist Office & Tourist Police: in Pothia (tel: (0243) 22100).

How to get there

Air: Connections from Athens.
Ferries: From Piraeus via Leros (12hrs), Kos (1hr) and Rhodes 4–6 times a week; from Patmos and Pserimos 3 times a week. Leros can also be reached by hydrofoil in summer from Kos, Rhodes, Patmos and Samos.

PATMOS ✓

Patmos is a holy isle and is invaded in summer by hordes of visitors and day-trippers. It is holy because here the apostle John heard the voice of God through cracks in the ceiling of a cave, and dictated to his disciple Prochorus the doom-laden prophetic poem the *Apocalypse*, which we call *Revelations*.

◆◆
KHORA (PATMOS TOWN)

Visitors come to see the cave, now a chapel, and to visit the Monastery of St John the Divine (Moní Ioannis Theologos), founded in 1088 by St Christodoulos, on a hill 2¾ miles (4km) south of the port of Skala. Buses go up the hill, but the hour's hard walk is rewarding for its superb views. The monastery was a town fortified against pirates so successfully that it has survived all those centuries of raids and invasions, from the Arabs to the Germans. It is still one of the richest religious houses in the world. Thirteenth-century frescos decorate the chapels. The library with thousands of rare old books is the most prized building, but you need the abbot's permission to see them. Scholars have 'borrowed' many priceless items over the centuries and they are now in national libraries in France, Germany and England. Zoodochos Pigi convent, built 1607, accepts visitors and has good frescos and ikons. Superb 17th-century mansions built by wealthy shipping magnates line twisting narrow streets, but they are usually shuttered and you cannot see their courtyards. They are used now by rich Athenians as holiday homes.

◆◆
SKALA

Skala is a pleasant little town with a busy square and small hotels and tavernas, calmer when the day visitors have gone. Two discos are discreet. Patmos has 14 miles (22.5km) of roads, and bus services are not bad, but walking is better. Motor-bikes are useful. Still better is to go on a caique trip.

Accommodation
Skala: **Patmion**, on the waterfront, B-class (tel: (0247) 31313). **Chris**, waterfront, C-class (tel: (0247) 31001). Grikou: **Xenia**, B-class (tel: (0247) 31219). **Flisvos**, D-class cheap, useful, (tel: (0247) 31380).

Restaurants
Victor Gouras' **Patmian House** in a Chora mansion serves superb food, but is pricey. There are good fish restaurants in Skala.

General information
Population 2,500
Area 13 sq miles (34 sq km)
163 nautical miles from Piraeus.
Police: harbour (tel: (0247) 31303).

How to get there
Ferries: From Piraeus (8hrs) Rhodes, Kos, Kalymnos and Leros 6 days a week; from Samos 3 times a week; from Ikaria once or twice weekly; May–September. Weekly Dodecanese island boat; daily caique to nearby island of Lipsi in summer.
Hydrofoils: in summer from Kos and Rhodes 3 times a week; Leros twice weekly.

One of the many medieval treasures to be seen in the fortified Monastery of St John on Patmos

NORTH SPORADES AND NORTH AEGEAN

SAMOS ✓

A pretty island only 1¾ miles (3km) from the Turkish coast, Samos was one of the first to accept charter holiday flights and is still popular with tourists. However, it is big enough not to look overcrowded, except in the port of Pythagorion when day-trippers arrive from Patmos. Its greenery comes from natural springs, but you will find most of its beauty inland, especially in the south, where there are pine woods, figs, olive groves and many vineyards. Samian wine has been famous through history. The sweet red is easy to get. Most of the dry white goes to Athens. Parts of the rocky north coast are inaccessible. Summer bus services are good but stop in the early evening.

◆◆
VATHI (SAMOS TOWN)

The main town and Piraeus ferry port, set in a U-shaped bay, is called Vathi, but the deep-port part is called Samos Town which has a fine archaeological museum. Restoration of elegant 19th-century buildings has improved its looks. Even the old part of Vathi on a steep hillside is still a working town not a tourist resort, though there are many pensions available.

◆◆
PYTHAGORION (PITHAGORION)

Rooms are hard to find in the other, much more attractive, port of Pythagorion 8 miles (13km) further south. It was

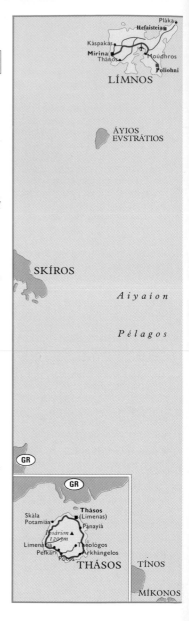

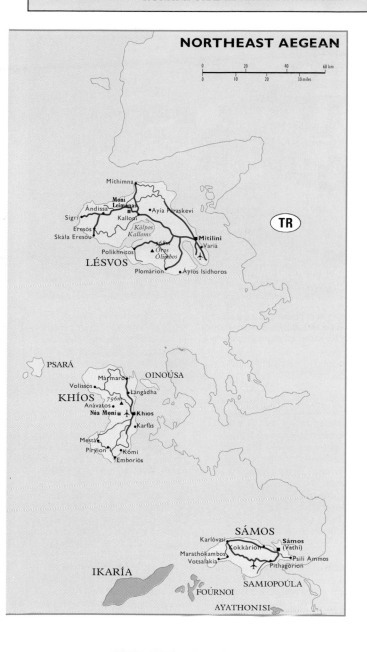

NORTHEAST AEGEAN

NORTH SPORADES AND NORTH AEGEAN

Who would think that the peaceful port of Pythagorion was once capital of the notorious pirate Polycrates

called Tigani, but the name was changed in 1955 in honour of the mathematician Pythagoras, who was born here in 6th century BC. It is still a fishing port, though smaller ferries call. The views across the Mycale Straits to Turkey are lovely, and the tree-lined harbourside, lined with tavernas, is very pleasant at night. There is a small sandy beach and a long pebbly beach beyond the harbour.

The tyrant-corsair Polycrates built the great mole on which the modern town is built, and a big tunnel nearly a mile (1.5km) north of the town, incredible for its time. Nearly 6½ft (2m) high and wide, and called Evpalinion after the engineer, it took thousands of slaves 15 years to build. It ran for two-thirds of a mile (1,000m) through the rock of Mount Kas, carried water to the city, and was used as a bolt-hole when the Persians attacked. It has collapsed in one place and unfortunately, it is no longer possible to explore it.

BEACHES

A pleasant place to stay, still an attractive fishing village, Kokari is on a bus route 6¼ miles (10km) from Vathi, with a long pebble beach lined with small tavernas. Ormos on the south coast is a delightful old-style Greek fishing and caique-building port. Over a headland about 1¼ miles (2km) away, is the nicest beach – Votsalakia – sand and pebble with shade. There are frequent buses to Samos Town 32 miles (52km) away. At Psili Ammos Marathokambos there is a super white-sand beach.

Accommodation

Vathi: **Hotel Samos**, 11 Sophouli Street, facing the harbour, is modern, clean, has rooms with wc, shower, and a restaurant, C-class (tel: (0273) 28377/8).
Xenia, also facing the harbour, is slightly superior, B-class (tel: (0273) 27463). Samos Town: of many pensions, **Ionia**, 5 Manoli Kalomiri, is friendly and reasonable (tel: (0273) 28782).
Kokari: **Kokkari Beach Hotel**, right on the shore, is comfortable, C-class (tel: (0273) 92263).
Pythagorion: many hotels and pensions, mainly booked by package tours in July/August.
Tarsanas, on the western sea front, by a pebble beach, is B-class (tel: (0273) 61162).

Restaurants

Dionysos restaurant on Sophouli esplanade in Samos port is clean, rather too neat for a Greek taverna, and serves good, genuinely Greek food. Pythagorion's waterfront has a big choice of eating places.

General information

Population 43,000
Area 184 sq miles (476 sq km)
175 nautical miles from Piraeus.
Tourist Police: 2 Sahtouri Street (tel: (0273) 27980).
Harbour police: (tel: (0273) 27318).

How to get there

Air: Many charter flights go direct from Western European countries in summer. There are 2–3 flights daily from Athens (1hr); from Chios twice weekly (35mins); from Lesbos 1–2 a week (55mins); in summer from Mykonos 1–4 a week (40mins) also Kos and Thessaloniki.

Ferries: From Piraeus, 3–8 a week (12hrs); from Ikaria 3–7 weekly (2½hrs); from Paros 3–4 weekly; from Chios 2 weekly (4¾hrs); from Lesbos (Mitilini), Limnos, Kavala (mainland), Kos, Syros, Leros, Kalymnos, Rhodes, Chalki, Karpathos, Kassos, Crete, (Sitia, Aghios Nikolaos), Santorini, Folegandros and Milos all once a week.

CHIOS (KHIOS)

You will not meet many other tourists on Chios. It is rich and does not go out of its way to encourage visitors. It grew rich on shipping, mastik for chewing-gum and varnish, and money brought back from the US by returning emigrants.

◆◆
CHIOS (KHIOS) TOWN

You find high-rise concrete apartments and office blocks in the big port, Chios Town, and many fast-food hamburger joints and smart plastic bars: more Athenian than Greek-Island style. But in the evenings there is the traditional quayside walkabout, with no room for cars or noisy motorbikes until the early hours, when they all rev up at once. The lanes and alleys in the market area are very Greek, too, and there is an old Turkish town within the walls of the fortress. There are bus routes to the south of the isle and buses run frequently in the summer from Chios Town as far as Pirgi and Mesta. In the north buses follow the coast to Mamaros. Langada, a delightful fishing village 11 miles (18km) from the port, is at the end of a bay backed by hills thick with pines. Anavatos, 7½ miles (12km) inland, is a medieval village up a steep mountainside to a ruined castle. A nearly vertical cliff hovers over a deep gorge. Three people live in the village. In 1822 the islanders joined the Greek independence fight. Of the 100,000 islanders, the Turks murdered 30,000 and took 45,000 into slavery. The 400 people of Anavatos threw themselves over the cliff to avoid, torture and enslavement. South from Chios Town is attractive countryside and villages, some, like Sklavia, with Genoese villas and gardens, and houses with watermills. The Genoese ruled Chios from 1261 to 1566.

On the coast is a very pleasant working fishing port, Kataraktis, with tavernas on its sea front. Further down is Emborios between hills in a narrow bay. It has good fish tavernas and an unusual and strangely attractive beach of black volcanic pebbles and sand. A track joins it to Komi, with clean sand and pebble beaches and three tavernas. Another rocky track north leads past a very sandy cove and small-boat harbour, to Aghios Ioannis, a fishing hamlet. Ferries go from Chios Town to the nearby islands of Oinoussai, where there is a medieval castle, tavernas and hotels, and Psara.

Attractive and decorative plasterwork in Chios Town, financed from the profits of mastik

PIRGI (PIRYION)

Pirgi, 17 miles (27km) from
Chios, is a superb medieval
village, centre of the mastik area.
Mastik is a resin tapped from
gashes made in lentisk trees. For
centuries it was used for
chewing-gum to sweeten the
breath and for making varnish.
Now cellulose is used, but mastik
is used for pharmaceutics, to
make a form of ouzo and as a
jelly-jam eaten on a spoon.
When the Turks took Chios from
Genoa in 1566, the girls of the
harems were hooked to
chewing-gum. So the mastik
farmers of Chios were given
special privileges. When the
Turks destroyed towns, villages
and crops in 1822 they left the
mastik villages alone.

The huge close-packed houses
of Pirgi formed a fortified wall
against pirates. Their stone walls,
doorways and windows are
framed with arches, and there
are more arches over the narrow
streets. On the first floors are
small open courtyards with steps
up to flat roofs. Balconies with
ironwork railings are decorated
with plants and flowers, and
thousands of housemartins and
swifts nest and swoop along the
streets. Most remarkable and
beautiful are the graffiti – black
and white geometric patterns
engraved with black sand into
the plaster. The 12th-century
church of Aghii Apostoli, with an
octagonal tower, is very
attractive. Inside are wall
paintings by a Cretan artist of
1665. The inhabitants of Pirgi
village preserve many of their
traditional customs, and many
still wear local dress.

MESTA

Best-preserved of several of
these medieval walled villages
is Mesta, 7½ miles (12km)
northwest of Pirgi and quieter but
with the same delightful Genoese
houses. Four have been restored
and made into small guesthouses
run by the National Tourist
Organisation of Greece. Several
others in a little alley off the main
square have been converted into
a delightful hotel.

NÉA MONÍ

The other great site of Chios is
Néa Moní monastery, 8½ miles
(14km) from Chios Town (buses
and excursions). Founded in
1042 when three hermit monks
discovered a miraculous ikon, it
was looted by the Turks in 1822,
and the monks all killed. The
bell tower and vault collapsed in
the 1881 earthquake. Some
beautiful mosaics, masterpieces
of religious art, have survived.
The church is restored and has
a 1900s bell tower. Nuns have
replaced the monks.

Accommodation

Chios Town: **Chandris Chios**,
by the sea at Prokimea, is the
local businessmen's meeting
place, B-class (tel: (0271)
25761/8). **Kyma**, next door to
Chandris, was built in Italian
style with a fine painted ceiling;
C-class (tel: (0271) 25551/3).
Mesta: **Lida**, B-class pension (tel:
(0271) 76217). Kambos: **Perivoli**
pension, B-class is quiet (tel:
(0271) 31513).

Restaurants

Best fish restaurants are at
Karfas, the nearest beach to

Chios Town. **Tassos Restaurant**, 6 Livanou Street, is popular.

General information

Population 50,000
Area 325 sq miles (841 sq km)
153 nautical miles from Piraeus.
Tourist Office: 11 Kanari Street
(tel: (0271) 24217).
Harbour Police: (tel: (0271) 22837).

How to get there

Air: Flights come from Athens at least twice daily (50mins); from Lesbos (40mins), Samos (35mins) and Mykonos (55mins) once or twice a week.

Ferries: From Piraeus 3–7 days a week (10hrs); from Samos (mainland) 2 times a week (4¾hrs); from Lesbos 3–7 days a week (4hrs); from Thessaloniki 2 days a week; from Limnos, Kavala (mainland), Ikaria, Leros, Kalymnos, Kos, Rhodes, Chalki, Karpathos, Kassos, Crete (Sitia, Aghios Nikolaos), Santorini, Folegandros and Milos once a week. Ferries go daily to Oinoussai, and 3 times a week to Psara (3¾hrs). Ferries also connect with Çesme (Turkey).

LESBOS (LESVOS) ✓

Third largest of the Greek isles, the Greek Government calls it Lesbos, British and US tour operators usually call it Lesvos and locals and ferry companies call it Mytilini. Few visitors go, perhaps because it is not easy to explore the island without long, tiring bus journeys or without hiring a car (the only way to see much of the island). And local people, though very friendly, are more interested in their 11,000 olive trees than tourism. They provide some of the best olive oil in the world. Ferries call at the capital Mytilini, an industrial town, but holiday-makers prefer Molyvos (Mithimna), a pretty, delightful fishing town two hours away by coach in the north. The two towns have feuded since Classical times. They are only 40 miles (64km) apart, but the linking paved road is tortuous and mountainous. The easier coast road collapsed in the dreadful winter of 1986-7. The local lyric poetess Sappho was responsible for the second meaning of the word Lesbian. She ran a school and wrote passionate verse to her female pupils. The Orthodox church in Constantinople banned and burned most of her poems.

◆◆◆
MYTILINI (MITILINI) TOWN

A busy town, it has two harbours divided by a peninsula topped by an attractive ruined castle, rebuilt by the Genoese in the 14th century. The north harbour is commercial. The south is mostly for fishing boats and yachts. The waterfront is the heart of the town, with banks, businesses, snack bars, hotels and restaurants. Mytilini beach is organised, with chairs, shade and a snack bar.

Museums and sites

Archaeological Museum: ancient sculptures and ceramics (open daily, except Monday; 08.30– 15.00hrs).
Byzantine Museum: in Philanthropic Society building, has fine ikons.
Old House, Mitropoleos Street: 19th-century island home, complete with working kitchen.

These three museums are all in Mytilini Town.

Teriad Museum, Varia, 2½ miles (4km) south of Mytilini: a superb museum, purpose-built by the Parisian art critic Teriad in the grounds of his house to show his private collection, which includes works by Chagall, Miro, Picasso, Le Corbusier and many others. Also 40 paintings by the local primitive folk-artist Theophilos, which Teriad arranged to have shown in the Louvre, Paris.

Theophilos Museum, Varia: born in 1873, Theophilos was a painting tramp, painting walls in churches, tavernas and houses in return for food and ouzo. Teriad persuaded him to paint on canvas. Among 86 works here are some wonderful primitive paintings of Greek Island scenes and people. He died in 1934. The Ancient Theatre on pine-forested heights north of Mytilini, was one of the biggest in Greece, with room for an audience of 15,000.

The 13th century Genoese fortress is well preserved, with views over the town to the Turkish mainland.

The road to Molyvos from Mytilini passes the big, almost landlocked bay of Geras, then goes over mountains to Kalloni, a market town known for its fishing village, Skala Kalloni, on the huge Gulf of Kalloni and renowned for sardines – a rarer fish today and mostly consumed by visitors. A large sand beach has some shady trees.

Just before Kalloni, 25 miles (40km) west of Mytilini, a road into the hills leads to Aghia Paraskevi, 17 miles (27km) west of Mytilini, where they breed

Molyvos: even modern fishing nets need to be repaired

white horses. You can see lovely white mares with black foals, which turn white later. Leimonos monastery (Moní Leimonas) (1523), north of Kalloni, comes under Mount Athos monks and bans women visitors. It has magnificent carvings and ikons.

♦♦♦
MOLYVOS (MITHIMNA)

Molyvos is a delightful partnership of fishing village and small tourist resort. The charming harbour, a 10 minute walk from the village, is filled with old-style wooden fishing caiques. Elegant stone houses with red roofs rise in very steep lanes and cobbled steps to the strong walls of a ruined Genoese castle, from which there are views to Turkey. In the town, cars are banished from 18.00hrs until dawn.

Tavernas along the waterfront serve a good choice of fish. Nassos, on a road leading up from the harbour, can offer lobster, sea bream, snapper, red mullet and swordfish, plus local island beef and lamb. Molyvos' long pebbly beach is a bit disappointing but buses and taxis go to the sandy beach of the quieter village Petra, 34 miles (55km) west of Mytilini, with the same cobbled streets and red-roofed houses, and tavernas in the main square. An unpaved road from Molyvos leads to Loutra Eftalos, 3½ miles (6km) north, a spa by the sea with very hot springs, a small beach, a taverna and two hotels, Alkeos and a Molyvos pension owned by the similarly-named hotel in Molyvos.

A paved but winding mountainous road from Kalloni leads to Andissa, a large mountainside village, and on to Sigri, 28 miles (45km) from Kalloni, a very quiet fishing village known for its lobsters. This is walkers' country, with several good beaches and a Turkish castle in good order.

The beautiful setting for a monastery and its grounds near Andissa

◆◆
ERESSOS (ERESOS)

Reached by a south fork after Andissa, 28 miles (45km) from Kalloni, the birthplace of Sappho is delightful, with a superb main square under a huge plane tree and lively market. The village resort Skala Eressos, 4½ miles (7km) from Eressos, is on a wide sand beach 1½ miles (2.5km) long and slowly

expanding. It even has a disco in season. Its main square is lined with tavernas and restaurants, and there are several hotels. Fishing boats supply the tavernas. A few package tourists stay in rooms and pensions. These places in the west of the isle can be reached by bus, but this is lengthy and a car is invaluable. Summer excursions from Mytilini and Molyvos do help. In the south of the island are some beautiful routes, with lovely mountain views, but they can be rough and some not only

(25km) from Mytilini, a village of old wooden houses with flowered balconies in steep cobbled streets on the slopes of Mount Olympos, in a gorgeous setting of apple orchards and woods of olives, plane, chestnut and pine. There is a 12th-century church with an ikon said to date from AD 803 and a medieval castle.

◆◆
PLOMARI (PLOMARION)
Another paved road from Mytilini rounds the gulf of Geras down the south coast to Plomari, second biggest town on the island, 43½ miles (70km) from Mytilini. It has an old town on one side, a new one on the other, both packed close down a hillside. A busy commercial port, with an active fishing fleet, it is now also a resort, with the best beach nearby at Aghios Isidoros. Plomari claims to make the best ouzo in Greece; Aphrodite, at 90% proof, may be the strongest.

have boulders but sheer drops, and they wriggle and turn sharply. Take local advice. A paved road goes west from Mytilini to Polychnitos, an elegant spa with a not very desirable beach on Kallonis Bay.
There is a better beach westward at Nyfida, 5½ miles (9km) from Polychnitos. The spa has five springs claimed to be the hottest in Europe (76°–87.6°C). A road south reaches Vatera, with a grey sand and shingle beach nearly 5 miles (8km) long, among orchards and vineyards, with pensions, rooms and tavernas. The Mytilini-Polychnitos road passes a tortuous road on the left to lovely Agiassos, 15½ miles

Accommodation
Mytilini: **Sappho** on the waterfront, Prokymea Kountourioti, has character but is a bit noisy, C-class (tel: (0251) 28415). **Blue Sea**, 91 Prokymea Kountourioti, convenient by the ferry quay end of harbour, is comfortable, B-class (tel: (0251) 23994/5). Molyvos: **Sea Horse Hotel**, harbour quay square, is a neat and popular B-class pension (tel: (0253) 71320/1). **Molyvos I**, very pleasant, near the beach, pension A-class (tel: (0253) 71386). **Poseidon**,2 Parodos Possidonos very nice B-class pension, only 6 rooms, so book (tel: (0253) 71570). B-class **Delphinia I** is 20 minutes walk away in the hills

(tel: (0253) 71315). **Alkeos** has good views and swimming, but is a mile (1.5km) uphill from any tavernas, B-class (tel: (0253) 71002). Eressos: **Sappho the Eressia**, 12 Theofrastou Skala, C-class (tel: (0253) 53233).

Restaurants
Lesbos is very well off for locally caught fish, local beef, lamb and vegetables. **Asteria** in Mytilini is good value. In Molyvos, **Nassos** on the road from the harbour, is exceptional for variety and quality. By the harbour, the **Sea Horse Hotel** restaurant and the next door taverna, **To Limani**, are very good and popular. At **Georgios** (with rooms) by the beach, you eat under vines.

Fishing boats, modern apartments and ancient walls at Limenas

General information
Population 88,600
Area 629 sq miles (1,630 sq km)
188 nautical miles from Piraeus.
Tourist Office: (tel: (0251) 42111).
Tourist Police: (tel: (0251) 22770).

How to get there
Air: Charters via some European countries. Up to six flights daily from Athens (45mins). From Thessalonika, 6–7 weekly (1hr 20mins); from Chios (40mins) and Samos (55mins) 1 or 2 a week; from Rhodes 3 weekly (1hr 20mins); from Lemnos 4 weekly. **Ferries**: From Piraeus (14hrs) 6 a week; from Chios 6 weekly; from Thessaloniki and Kavala, Lemnos and Samnos twice weekly; once a week from Leros, Karpathos, Santorini, Crete, Folegandros and Milos.

LEMNOS (LIMNOS)

Near Turkey and opposite the Dardanelles, Lemnos, 185 sq miles (479 sq km), population 18,000, is a big military base and unexciting to travellers. Aircraft seats from Athens are often booked weeks ahead by military families. Seats are easier to obtain on flights from Lesbos (daily, 45mins). Mainland ferries from Kavala, Rafina and Thessaloniki. Myrina, capital and ferry port, is dominated by a Venetian castle with wonderful views of Mount Athos 34¾ miles (56km) away. The most pleasant scenery is in the southwest wine-growing area around Thanos.

THASSOS (THASOS)

A softly beautiful, languid island of hot sun and the smell of pines, protected from meltemi winds by the mainland of Macedonia only 6¾ miles (11km) away. Thassos is a round mountain covered with trees and little valleys where rivers run down to hidden coves or long sandy beaches, backed by olive groves, vineyards, wheat fields and vegetables.
There is plenty of accommodation because it has long lured Greeks from the mainland, but few foreigners go.

◆◆
LIMENAS (THASOS TOWN)

Like Kos Town, Limenas has ancient remains mixed up with its modern buildings, and many are lovely, for the central peak, Ipsarion, is virtually a block of marble. The main excavations:
● **The Agora**: Entered from beside the museum, there are remains from the classical city, of passageways, shops,

monuments, and an elaborate temple to Artemis. Buy a guide book, as there is little labelling.
● **The Ancient Theatre**: Set dramatically among pines overlooking a wide expanse of sea, the theatre is reached by steep steps. Performances in Greek of ancient drama are given on Saturdays from late-July to mid-August.
● **Ancient Walls**: Exploring means a strenuous 3 mile (5km) walk past the theatre. You can follow the walls past the foundations of a 5th-century temple to Apollo and a small sanctuary with a relief of Pan and his goats. The 'Secret Stairs' carved into rock in the 6th century BC lead to the Gateway of Silenus, the phallic god. His massive phallus (a fertility totem) was chiselled away in the 1930s during one of those 'moral cleansing' campaigns dictators have forced on Greeks.
● **The Museum**: This contains many archaeological finds, including interesting items from the temple of Artemis.
The town has a nice fishing harbour, and typically Greek shops and tavernas.

INLAND VILLAGES AND BEACHES

The most attractive inland village is Panagia, 7½ miles (12km) from Limenas, and set among trees and springs on the slopes of the mountain, with delightful sea views. At Christi Akti, a tiny resort also called Skala Potamias, you can taste the local catch outside the tavernas. At Archangelos round the coast, 23½ miles (38km) south of Limenas, is a convent where nuns show visitors the hollows in the stone made, they claim, by St Luke kneeling in prayer. The road continues round the coast to Potos, a small but growing resort by a big beach, with plenty of tavernas, small modern blocks of apartments, a comfortable modern hotel. A road through a lovely valley leads to the old capital, Theologos. Here you can buy Thasian honey. Pefkari, a smaller village a mile (1.5km) from Potos, has a sand beach but rocky seabed. Beyond is Limenaria, an overgrown fishing village, which still has a strong German flavour as a legacy from a company which mined ore here before the 1914 war. Quiet by day, it wakes up at night to bar music and discos. Thassos has one fault – mosquitoes. But modern devices deal with them at night. Forest fires are a hazard, too. But it is a lovely, truly Greek, isle.

Accommodation

Limenas: **Lena**, Megalou Alexandrou, is a clean, comfortable modern hotel with balconies, all rooms with wc, shower, E-class (tel: (0593) 22793). Among dozens of others, **Timoleon**, Paralia (waterfront near the ferry quay) is pleasant, B-class (tel: (0593) 22177); **Akti**, is cheaper, clean, B-class pension (tel: (0593) 22326). A recommended A-class hotel is **Roula** (tel: (0593) 22905). **Makryammos Bungalow Hotel** on the private beach is A-class (tel: (0593) 22101). Limenaria: plenty of choice. **Hatzichristos**, vine clad and pleasant, on the beach is better than its rating; all rooms with

wc, E-class (tel: (0593) 51567). **Menel**, 43 Omonias is good value, C-class (tel: (0593) 51396).

Restaurants

One of the best restaurants in Limenas is **Akrogiali** at the end of the esplanade away from the old harbour: good food.

General information

Population 16,000
Area 146 sq miles (379 sq km)
Tourist Office & Tourist Police: Limenas (tel: (0593) 22500). Harbour Police: (tel: (0593) 71290).

How to get there

Air: To Keramoti (mainland) then ferry (see below).
Ferries: From Kavala (mainland, 1hr 15mins) daily; from Keramoti (mainland, 35mins) 12 a day, every hour in summer, 7 a day in winter.

SPORADES

SKIATHOS ✓

Skiathos is one of the most beautiful of the Greek islands. It has gentle hills, pine and olive groves down to the sea, dense woods covering whole areas in green, long sandy beaches and wild shores, with western mountains so rugged that you can enter only on foot or mule. All this is packed into an island 8 miles (13km) long. But it is the fine beaches which have made it popular for holidays for so long – those and the big airfield built in the 1960s. Charters flew to Skiathos from all over Europe long before many visitors had airfields. With the visitors have come good restaurants and a wide choice of nightlife.

BEACHES

All round the island are sweeps of clean yellow sand. Most beaches have tavernas and restaurants, even Megas Aselinos on the west coast, which can be reached only on foot or by caique.

Koukounaries, 7½ miles (12km) southwest of Skiathos Town, has one of the best stretches of sand in Greece – 1,094 yds (1,000m), backed by shady pines. In season a water-skiing school disturbs the calm of this tranquil spot.

A footpath from the road behind Koukounaries lagoon leads to a lovely sand beach, Mandraki, in the Bay of Xerxes.

You must take a caique from Skiathos port to Lalária in the north (1hr), where there is a dramatic beach of silver pebbles enclosed by sheer grey-white rock cliffs.

KASTRO

A path marked by red blobs of paint across Skiathos, which you can pick up at Aghios Konstantinos on the edge of Skiathos Town, takes you in 2½-3 hours to the crumbling walls of Kastro, the old Byzantine fortified town on a point with superb views. In the 16th century it had 300 houses, 22 churches and was a refuge for the island's whole population against pirates. Now all that remains is an entrance gateway, two ruined churches and a hammam (Turkish baths).

SKIATHOS TOWN

Buses are frequent on the coast road to and from Skiathos Town. Taxis cruise and the shared cost is reasonable.

Skiathos port is lively. It is divided into two by an island now joined to the mainland by a bridge. The Venetian castle, heavily restored, is a school. The original port is used by fishing boats, the main port by ferries and cargo boats. Cars and people cram the streets in summer. The harbourside tavernas have a rather noisy happy atmosphere at night. Up

SPORADES

The fine beaches of Skiathos have made the island popular for a long time with discerning holiday-makers

the steps at the south end of the harbour are tiny, delightful crowded fish tavernas.

Accommodation
Prices drop heavily off-season. Skiathos Town: **Kostis**, Evangelistrias Street, is dearer than most pensions and better (tel: (0427) 42979). **Hotel Akti** on the waterfront is good value, C-class (tel: (0427) 22024). Koukounaries Beach: **Skiathos Palace**, expensive by island standards, Luxury-class (tel: (0427) 22242). The **Xenia** costs about half as much, B-class (tel: (0427) 22041/2).

Restaurants
There is a high standard of meals in many tavernas and restaurants, with good prawns and crab dishes. **Miramare** is the most popular on the waterfront.

General information
Population 4,100
Area 18½ sq miles (48 sq km)
Tourist Office & Tourist Police: (tel: (0427) 21111).
Harbour Police: (tel: (0427) 22017).

How to get there
Air: Many charters fly direct from Europe. There are 3–7 flights a day from Athens (50mins).
Ferries: Daily from Volos on the mainland (5½hrs), where there are bus connections down to Athens; daily from Aghios Konstandinos (3¼hrs); 1–3 a week from Kimi on Evia (5¼hrs); from Skopelos (½hr) and Alonnisos (2½hrs) 1 or 2 a day; 1–4 a week from Skyros.
Hydrofoils: Daily from Aghios Konstandinos, Volos and, occasionally, Nea Moudania in Halkidiki.

SKOPELOS ✓

Though Skopelos port becomes more sophisticated every year and the flow of visitors grows, Skopelos remains the dreamy, undeveloped Greek Isle of 30 years ago. It still has very few roads with only one bus route, and to explore it you must use boats as buses and walk goat tracks over hills covered with trees – pine and plane, silver-leafed olives, almonds, quinces and plums, whose fruit is made into prunes. It is a beautiful isle, especially in spring time.

◆◆
SKOPELOS TOWN

The town of Skopelos is beautiful, too. Known locally as Chora, it is built on a steep amphitheatre around a busy port used by fishing boats, supply caiques and yachts, its quay lined with café tables. Along white-paved streets, houses with roofs of blue slate and red tiles rise to a Venetian castle. Houses tend to be taller than on most isles and their blue and green shutters and balconies with flowers bring colour to the intense whiteness. Among them are Venetian houses with projecting upper storeys held by wooden beams and internal courtyards. There are 123 churches in the town, some so small that you might mistake them for cottages. The Venetian castle was used by the pirate Philip Gizi, who made his base here until he was captured. In the War of Independence it was headquarters for leaders of the Greek insurrection against the

Turks. The dusty road to the now ruined fort is the home of goats and donkeys. The view is superb.
Hotels and a few discos are mostly hidden on the far side of the bay. The main nightly entertainment is walking in volta along the quayside, then eating and drinking in a taverna where someone may play an instrument.

◆◆
LOUTRAKI (LOUTRAKION)

Loutraki has an enormous ferry quay, looking odd beside the little fishing village with boats pulled up on the shingle. Except when a ferry is due, it is a quiet, calm place, where you can sit outside one of the tavernas with a cooling drink and a book and be at peace with the world. The ferry quay was built here, because Glossa, in woods up the hill, a beautiful place, is an important agricultural centre. Built mostly under the Turks, its white and ochre houses survived the 1965 earthquake. Chickens, donkeys and goats seem to have taken over the dusty cobbled alleys. There is one taverna and a small hotel, the Avra (tel: (0424) 33550). A mule track from Makhalos, a village south of Glossa, takes you to the church of Aghios Ioannis on the rugged north coast. It is reached by 100 steps in the rock and is perched like an eagle's nest over the sea.

MONASTERIES

Skopelos has 360 churches and several monasteries. Four are within walking distance of Skopelos Town. Aghia Varvara is fortified; it contains 15th-century frescos. Moni

Evangelistrias has wonderful
views. It has a dozen nuns and
is open to viewing – ironic, for it
was founded by the monks of
Mount Athos who still ban all
women from their monastery.
Prodromos, looking out from a
craggy height to the isle of
Alónissis, still has nuns in
residence. Metamorphosis,
recently abandoned as a
monastery, is used for a big
August festival.
Skopelos is superb at the end of
May and early June – quiet, not
too hot and very green.

Accommodation
There are about 34 hotels in
Skopelos Town, mostly seasonal.
Amalia is B-class with 50
bedrooms (tel: (0424) 22688);
Aeolos has 79 bedrooms, C-
class (tel: (0424) 22233).

Restaurants
Good fish is served in waterfront
tavernas at Skopelos Town and
Loutraki. In Glossa, **Rania**
restaurant has good views.

General information
Population 4,500
Area 36½ sq miles (95 sq km)
Tourist Office & Tourist Police:
(tel: (0424) 22235).
Harbour Police: (tel: (0424)
22180).

How to get there
Ferries: Most people fly to
Skiathos, then take the boat.
Ferries from the mainland call at
Skopelos Town and Loutraki
(Glossa). There are ferries daily
from Volos (4½hrs), where
there are bus connections to
Athens; daily from Aghios
Konstandinos (4½hrs); 1–3
weekly from Kimi (Evia, 3½hrs);
from Alónissos 1–2 a day (½hr);
from Skiathos daily (½hr); 1–4
weekly from Skyros; from
Lemnos 1–2 a week (7hrs).
Hydrofoils: Daily from Aghios
Konstandinos and Volos.

*A dramatically-sited church on
Skopelos: one of at least 360
churches on the island*

PEACE AND QUIET

Wildlife and Countryside in the Greek Islands
By Paul Sterry

With unbelievably blue seas, a wonderful climate and delightful sandy beaches, the islands are a holiday-maker's paradise. They also have a rich variety of wildlife and, despite increased tourism and development, there is much to see off the beaten track as well as in the resorts themselves. The character and climate of the islands lying to the west of the mainland in the Ionian Sea are very different from those to the east in the Aegean, the rugged Ionian Isles having almost twice as much annual rainfall as the Aegean Isles. Throughout the islands, however, most rainfall occurs during the winter months and it is almost unheard of to have a cloudy day during the summer. Summer temperatures rise to highs of around 35°C (95°F), which causes problems of sunburn for the people, but also has a profound effect upon the plants and animals of the region. Winter is a time for growing, and early spring the time to reproduce. Consequently, most of the flowers bloom and wither by June and many animals go into a state of summer hibernation called 'aestivation' to avoid the searing heat.

The Coasts and Seas

Because the Mediterranean is more or less land-locked, it differs from most of the world's other seas and oceans in having a minimal tidal range. This is extremely convenient for the holiday industry because it

Audouin's gulls visit harbours and ports around the coasts

means that the beaches are always accessible. However, it also means that very few inter-tidal animals and plants can live on the shoreline, although the sea has a wealth of life.

The productivity of the seas around the Greek Islands is rich indeed, as witnessed by the menus in the tavernas. The fish, squid and crustaceans are also eaten by some specialised oceanic animals. Schools of fish-eating dolphins are seen from boats, and these playful marine mammals often come close to vessels out of curiosity. Dolphins may be quite common in the eastern Mediterranean, but not so the Mediterranean monk seal. Once persecuted by fishermen to the point of extinction, they are now rarely seen despite their immense size, their numbers having dwindled to a handful which frequent isolated coasts and islets. In the summer, the females produce their calves in inaccessible sea caves

PEACE AND QUIET

While on boat trips you may also see flocks, known as 'rafts', of shearwaters, truly oceanic birds that fly in long lines with stiffly held wings. The brownish, eastern Mediterranean race of the Manx shearwater is sometimes joined by its larger cousin, the Cory's shearwater, which resembles a miniature albatross.

On inaccessible cliffs and islets, Audouin's gulls occasionally nest. These rare and elegant seabirds resemble a small herring gull, but have a red beak and dark legs as adults. Outside the breeding season, they often wander around the coast and visit ports where the juvenile birds can be a challenge to identify.

Loggerhead turtles still try to nest on remote sandy beaches on some of the Aegean Islands. Their eggs, which lie buried in the sand, sometimes prove an irresistible temptation for beech martens, curious members of the weasel family which are named after the tree rather than the habitat. Although normally creatures which prefer the cover of wooded hillsides, they can occasionally be seen on quiet beaches at dawn.

Insects

For much of the year, insect life abounds on the Greek Islands. Colourful butterflies visit the flowers of the maquis and a myriad of beetles and bugs scurry for cover. As with the flower plants, the spring is the most productive time of year to look for insects. There is plenty of vegetation for the adults to lay their eggs on and flowers to provide energy-giving nectar. Among the butterflies, the clouded yellow is a familiar sight all around the Mediterranean and particularly so in the Greek Islands, being a widespread breeding species and a famous migrant. Similarly renowned for their powers of migration are the Bath white and the Queen of Spain fritillary, the latter with beautiful metallic spangles on its underwing.

The southern festoon is a speciality of Greece and its islands. Since its caterpillar's foodplant is birthwort, a plant which prefers shade, the butterflies are most commonly found around open woodlands and glades. Their amazingly colourful wings are reminiscent of a stained-glass window.

Although seldom seen by day, moths are also abundant and are commonly drawn to lighted windows after dark. Most spectacular of these are the hawk moths, which sometimes feed from garden flowers at

The oleander hawk moth is a large and colourful species

dusk. The oleander hawk moth is one of the largest and most attractive species and, as its name suggests, its caterpillars feed on the poisonous, ornamental shrub oleander and are impressive in their own right. During the height of the summer, insects are at their least numerous. However, a few species of butterfly brave the heat, but most have died off leaving their chrysalids to survive until the rains of autumn. Grasshoppers and bush-crickets are still conspicuous to the eye and to the ear, and are incredibly active in the heat.

The summer is the season for cicadas, which sing incessantly from every tree and bush on the islands. They are most impressive ventriloquists and it is almost impossible to locate them by their sound. The easiest way to see them is to look for the mud turrets which the underground larval stages make just prior to emergence. By careful observation, the emerging adults can sometimes be found early in the morning.

Reptiles and Amphibians

Being cold-blooded animals not able to maintain their body temperature, reptiles and amphibians are highly dependent upon warmth from the sun. The colder the temperature, the less active they are, and as a result, some species hibernate during the colder winter months.

With warm springs and hot summers, the islands are ideal for reptiles, and snakes and lizards abound. Because water

Although not venomous, large whip snakes look menacing

is at a premium during the summer, frogs, toads and newts, which need standing water in which to breed, are far less frequent. However, the hardy green toad occurs on some of the Cyclades and the green tree frog croaks around the smallest of pools.

The best time of year to look for snakes and lizards is in the spring. Many will have just emerged from hibernation and lie about soaking up the sun's rays. Because reptiles become more active as they get hotter, search for them early in the morning; later in the day they retreat under cover to avoid overheating. During the summer months, when the temperatures can be excessively hot, even for a cold-blooded creature, many switch from hunting by day to a nocturnal lifestyle, and so torchlight forays can then be productive.

Tortoises are the most endearing reptiles found in the

PEACE AND QUIET

Greek Islands, and are certainly the easiest to see. The most widespread species in the Ionian Islands is Hermann's tortoise. Elsewhere in the region, it has probably been introduced along with other tortoise species. In the spring, they are a familiar sight as they rustle through scrubby vegetation. Regrettably, they are often killed by cars, so if you see one trying to cross the road, help it across.

Lizards abound. Geckos are frequent visitors to villas, and scurry over almost every rock face. Green lizards are common on some of the islands like Thassos, and are fond of baking in bare, open areas close to cover.

Lizards form a major part of the diet of the numerous snakes. One of the largest and most impressive of these is the large whip snake, a handsome reptile which may reach a length of 6½ ft (2m) and haunts rocky hillsides and olive groves. They are frequently seen crossing the road, so drive carefully to avoid running them over.

Scrub and Woodland

At first glance, away from the coasts, most of the islands look barren and inhospitable. Typically the soil is dry and stony with small shrubs interspersed with patches of low-growing plants. Their leaves are usually leathery or waxy, to resist desiccation, and plants are often spiny to discourage grazing animals. Do not be fooled, however, by the apparent paucity and uniformity in the vegetation, because over 200 species of

flower have been found in this type of habitat. In April and May, vetches, brooms, lavenders and asphodels put on a fine display of colour, but in July, the whole landscape, with the exception of the shrubbery, evergreen plants, will have turned a uniform brown.

In some senses, this barren phrygana habitat – as the botanists call it – as well as the more shrubby maquis, are man-made environments, or at least man-influenced. Before colonisation, most of the islands would have been covered by evergreen woodland to an altitude of about 3,280ft (1,000m). These woodlands have gradually been cleared over the centuries and the soils, often too poor to permit full regeneration of the forests, have developed into the typical scrubby habitats we see today. Some of the islands, such as those in the northern Aegean, still have extensive woodlands, and remnants exist on many others, where the dominant tree is the aleppo pine. The open woodland that it forms allows plenty of shrubby and herbaceous plants to grow underneath, and some of them predominate in the cleared habitats as well. Tree heather, strawberry tree, juniper and laurel contribute to the understorey, and several species of rock-roses attract butterflies to their flowers.

The kermes oak, with leaves like those of a miniature holly, is typical of the scrubby phrygana habitat, but also occurs in the shade of maquis and any remnants of aleppo pine woodland. Like the olive trees with which it often grows, it provides cover for nesting birds such as the Ruppell's warbler. This delightful songster has a pronounced, white 'moustache', which separates its black hood and throat. Although common on almost all the islands, it is not at all widespread on the mainland.

Agricultural Land
Most Greek Islands are fringed by coastal alluvial plains, and the fertile, loamy soil is perfect for cultivation. Even comparatively barren and stony soils are now coming under the plough, being used to grow vines and other hardy plants. Apart from the crops themselves, these cultivated areas support a variety of birds and insects, and are particularly rewarding if they are irrigated.

Surprisingly few of the crop-producing shrubs, trees and woody plants of the islands are actually native to the region. Figs, pomegranates and olives all probably came from the Middle East, and even the grape-vine probably came from Asia. Some plants have even more exotic origins, with oranges and peaches coming from China and peppers and tomatoes from the New World. However, all these plants needed very little encouragement and now thrive throughout the Mediterranean. Like many of the native species, the cultivated plants generally grow during the mild, wet winter months. This gives them a head-start before the onset of the hot, dry summer. Many of the blossom trees, such as almond and apricot, flower from December to January, and oranges bear ripe fruit from the start of the new year. Cultivated fields can be excellent areas for the birdwatcher on the Greek Islands. Almond trees and fruit groves provide shade from the sun and nesting sites for birds such as serins. Shrikes are common visitors to orchards

Black-eared wheatears are boldly marked and alert birds

PEACE AND QUIET

and drop to the ground the instant they see a rustling insect or lizard. Several species pass through the islands on migration, and red-backed shrikes occasionally nest. They have the rather gruesome nickname 'butcher birds', after their habit of impaling their prey on thorns or barbed wire.

Fields around the coast can be thronged with small birds during the spring migration and several species stay to nest. Black-eared wheatears, resplendent in their black, fawn and white plumage, hop from rock to rock in search of insects. Short-toed larks, on the other hand, creep around slowly, looking more like mice than birds. They seem to have a natural ability to keep to the furrows and scraps of vegetation and can be very difficult to spot. For all their apparent secrecy, they are not especially shy, and will sometimes walk right up to a quiet and stationary observer.

Hills and Mountains

Although best known for their coasts, many Greek Islands have hills and mountains rising above 3,280ft (1,000m). Among the highest at 5,315ft (1,620m), is Mount Ainos on Cephalonia, lying within the boundaries of a national park. Like most other mountains in the Ionian Isles, it is composed of limestone, which encourages an interesting flora to develop. The hillsides have often been cleared of woodland and are heavily grazed by goats. This exposes flowering plants to the baking sun throughout the year,

Greek silver firs still cloak mountain tops in Cephalonia

and because the soils are often dry and porous, only hardy species like squills, irises, crocuses and star-of-Bethlehem can survive. These flower from March to May, looking quite out of place in the stony soil. Pride of place, however, goes to the orchids which abound on the hills of the Greek Islands and the varieties of tongue and bee orchids are a major attraction for botanists in spring. Mountain-tops above 3,280ft (1,000m) are sometimes still covered by coniferous woodland. In Ionian islands like Cephalonia, the dominant tree is the Greek silver fir, a speciality of the region. Only shade-tolerant plants can grow under its dense canopy, but hellebores, cyclamens and squills might all be found. During the summer, rocky hillsides on almost all the Greek

Islands are the haunt of Cretzschmar's buntings. With their brick-red plumage and blue head, these attractive little birds are another speciality of the region. In the skies above, griffon and Egyptian vultures may soar overhead, on the look-out for carrion, and they are often joined by that most spectacular of fliers, the alpine swift. With its striking, pied plumage, this master of the air is half as big again as the common swift.

Bird Migration

Most of the islands have far fewer breeding bird species than adjacent area on the mainland. This is due in part to the rugged nature of the landscape and uniformity of the terrain. Freshwater marshes and extensive areas of natural woodland are unusual and so the resident birds tend to be species which prefer open country. Visit during spring or autumn migration, however, and the numbers and varieties of species to be found increase dramatically. Many birds from northern Europe spend the winter south of the Mediterranean, and pass through Greece on their way back north in the spring. In April and May, when the winds are from a favourable southerly direction, thousands of small birds will pass through the islands. If conditions remain good for migration, most will stay only briefly, but if the wind direction changes or a front passes over, they may stay and feed for a longer period. Common and black-eared wheatears, black redstarts and

tawny pipits frequent sandy fields where they search the furrows for insects. They are commonly joined by flocks of turtle doves who peck at seedheads and flowers, while in the skies above, colourful and noisy flocks of bee-eaters glide their way northwards. Autumn migration is less pronounced than in spring, but goes on for longer, so from July until October, adult birds and their offspring drift down through the islands. During July and August, brilliant blue rollers are a conspicuous feature as they perch on wires and bushes, ever alert for passing insects. Young birds of all species are generally less skilled at navigation, so you are more likely to find unusual species at this time of the year. The islands play host to a most unusual bird of prey. During the summer, the cliffs are the haunt of Eleanora's falcons, whose mastery of the air enables them to catch other birds on the wing. Unlike most other European birds, they nest in the autumn, which may at first seem rather peculiar. However, they take advantage of the vast numbers of migrant songbirds passing through Greece in the autumn, and consequently their young seldom go short of food.

Turtles

Long before European tourists discovered the sandy beaches of Greece, they were visited by loggerhead turtles. For these superbly adapted marine reptiles, their visits to dry land are not recreational, but are a matter of necessity for the survival of the species.

PEACE AND QUIET

For most of the year, loggerheads are found in the deeper Mediterranean waters, where they feed mainly on jellyfish. During spring and early summer, however, they move into shallower water and are often seen from small boats. When they judge the time is right, the females come ashore to lay their eggs in the sand. Although superbly adapted to the marine environment, with powerful flippers and a streamlined shell, they are lumbering and vulnerable on land and to avoid predators they come ashore only at night. After dragging herself up the beach, the female turtle digs a deep hole in the sand in which she lays her eggs. When the clutch is completed, it is covered over with sand and the eggs are left to their fate. Although the whole process may take several hours, egg-laying is almost always finished before dawn and the only

Loggerhead turtles hatching on a secluded sandy beach

indication that the beach has been visited will be tell-tale tracks in the sand to and from the sea. The speed at which the eggs develop depends upon the temperature of the sand, but generally takes a couple of months. Then during September or October a remarkable thing happens. Early one morning the sand will erupt as all the hatchlings from a nest burst out of the ground and rush to the sea. Unfortunately, many do not even make it to the water, falling prey to various predators, and of those that do, only one or two survive to adulthood.

Turtles are easily discouraged from egg-laying by lights or noise, so it is not surprising that they have deserted many of their ancestral beaches. Nests are also frequently raided by dogs or pigs, or even by man, and so now the turtles only visit a few remote beaches. Fortunately, the Greek authorities are aware of the conflict of interests between turtles and tourists and some beaches on islands like Cephalonia and Zakynthos are protected for the turtles' benefit. With care and caution, these great animals can be watched at close quarters, and in the future this in itself could become a real tourist attraction.

Spring Flowers

Mediterranean summers may suit holiday-makers, but they present real difficulties for the flowering plants of the region. The hot, dry climate causes problems with desiccation, and much of the woodland which would have provided shade has

Wildlife Highlights of the Greek Islands

● **Cephalonia** – loggerhead turtles nest on a few, undisturbed beaches in May and June. Forested Mount Ainos has Greek silver firs, woodland birds and birds of prey.
● **Zakinthos** – nesting loggerhead turtles on a few beaches. Excellent open country habitat for birds and flowers in the early spring.
● **Lesbos** – unspoilt island close to the Turkish coast. Habitats include woodland, open country, agricultural land and saltpans. Special birds include Kruper's nuthatch and cinereous bunting, both absent from other islands. A wide variety of other species.
● **Naxos** – wonderful mountain scenery and rich agricultural lowlands. Good for birds and spring flowers and one of the greener Greek Islands.

Flowers like the yellow bee orchid abound in spring

been cleared. To add to this, the soils are porous, so any rain that does fall soon soaks away. Not surprisingly, the plants that are most successful are those with underground storage systems such as rhizomes or bulbs. During the comparatively mild and wet winters, they produce leaves, grow and store food underground and eventually flower in the spring. For a brief period, from March to May, the landscape looks green and colourful, but thereafter the leaves wither away and by July, all the vegetation, with the exception of the evergreen shrubs, has turned a uniform brown. The food stored in the bulbs and rhizomes is enough to see the plants through to the autumn. The best areas for spring flowers are the open phrygana and maquis type habitats. Rock-roses, with their waxy leaves and crinkly flowers, provide shelter for low-growing squills, crocuses, iris and daffodils and many of the flowers, such as the grape hyacinths, will be familiar as cultivated forms to gardeners. Orchids are common on almost all the islands and it is not unusual to notch up a dozen species or more in a single week. Spectacular species like the bug orchid, with its strong-smelling flowers, and the naked man orchid are widespread, but for sheer variety, the bee orchid family are clear winners. Although all the bee orchids conform to a basic pattern – with

PEACE AND QUIET

a large, rounded lower flower-lip – the diverse shapes, colours and forms are astonishing. Some, like the yellow bee orchid, are widespread in the Mediterranean region while others, such as the Greek spider orchid, are restricted to Greece and its islands.

The onset of autumn in the Mediterranean is not accompanied by the die-back in vegetation so familiar in northern Europe. Instead, the milder, wetter climate following the oppressive summer induces a form of second spring. It becomes green again and new sets of flowers begin to bloom.

Seasonal Wildlife Highlights Throughout the Greek Islands

● **March** – first flush of spring flowers and insects appears in the fields and open country.

● **April** – best month for flowers and especially orchids. Migrant birds start passing through the region. Bird song can be heard in scrub and olive groves.

● **May** – late bird migrants such as bee-eaters appear. Late-flowering plants are in bloom, earlier species having begun to die back and turn brown.

● **June** – most annual flowers have withered and turned brown. Snails begin to cluster on dry stems - 'aestivating' or resting through the dry summer. Colourful butterflies abound. Turtles nest on remote beaches.

● **July** – a quiet month for land birds and flowers. Seabirds can be seen on many of the ferry crossings. Such as between mainland Greece (Kylini) and Cephalonia and Zakinthos, or Naxos to Paros and Mykonos to Ermupolis or Tinos.

● **August** – Eleanora's falcons feed on returning migrant birds around the coasts and cliffs of the Greek Islands. Rollers – bright blue birds – are a familiar sight on many islands.

● **September** – migrant bird numbers are at their highest. Bad weather induces birds to become grounded. A flush of autumn-flowering plants appear.

Bird Trapping

Early autumn, tens of millions of songbirds fly south from northern Europe to Africa for the winter. As they pass through the Mediterranean countries, millions of them never make it any further, falling victim to the 'sportsmen;' of the region. Similar tactics are also employed towards the songbirds which, like, the song thrush, spend the winter in the mild climate of Greece and its islands.The methods employed by the hunters are varied. Guns are used against birds of prey and herons, while nets, traps and snares are used for small birds. Perhaps most insidious of all is the technique of liming twigs and branches, where a sticky glue holds the victim's feet until it either dies of starvation or is collected by the hunter.

Some of the birds which die in Greece are killed for no better reason than to be served as delicacies, while others are sacrificed in the name of 'sport'. Fortunately, this pursuit is widely publicised outside Greece, and in response to public opinion the authorities will hopefully implement restrictive legislation.

SHOPPING AND SOUVENIRS

Most smaller isles have 'supermarkets', which are really little serve-yourself grocer's shops. They sell drinks including ouzo and wine. Bakers normally sell pies, especially cheese, and simple cakes. Seasonal tourist shops sell postcards, 'Greek' clothes made for tourists (similar on every island, but often attractive), and sometimes such specialist clothes as hand-knitted sweaters. Simple wool sweaters can be cheap even by British standards, and some are oiled for fishermen. But they are not fashionable or sophisticated in any way. Jewellery on these islands is imported from Athens and Mykonos. Mykonos sells gold jewellery at inflated prices. You can see a few last potters at work on Siphnos.

Apart from clothes, wine and liqueur, the tourist shops offer pottery and ceramics, hand-woven carpets and cloth, long-haired rugs (*flokati*), genuinely embroidered clothes (usually in old-fashioned styles), lace, carved or turned wooden ornaments, 'Greek' shoulder bags, sponges (Kalymnos is the 'sponge isle'), reproduction ikons, jewellery in ceramics, gold or silver, marble or onyx carvings, and worry beads (*komboloi*). Also many sell honey and pistachio nuts. There is little outstanding to bring home as souvenirs: it is entirely a matter of cost and taste.

A typical souvenir of a Greek island holiday is a string of 'worry beads'

FOOD AND DRINK

Greek food may not always be the best in the world, but the views from taverna tables can make up for it

FOOD AND DRINK

*(Please refer to the **What to See** section for restaurants and each island's speciality, where applicable)*

Eating is very much a happy social occasion, rather than a serious gourmet experience, and no-one goes to Greece for the food or wine. Dishes are mostly Turkish in origin, as in all the Balkans occupied for long by the Turks, but never mention this to the Greeks. Nor does Turkish Delight exist. It is 'Greek Delight'. Surprisingly few spices are used in Greek food, but they use quite a lot of herbs, especially oregano. You

notice little salt and pepper, so popular dishes can seem a little tasteless, like meatballs (*kefthedes*) and cheese pie (*tiropita*, often bought hot from the bakers for a meal or snack). Other popular pastry pies include chicken (*kotopita*), spinach (*spanakopita*), courgette (*kolokithopita*) and the expensive favourite lamb (*arnaki*).

Fish

It is advisable to like fish when visiting the Greek Islands. It is nearly always good, often superb, bought as it is landed and sometimes in the pan within 2 or 3 hours. Prices have gone up for three reasons – over-fishing, more tourists to feed and high prices paid by Athens restaurants tempting islanders to export. Mostly fish is grilled and, alas, sometimes over grilled in tavernas where the family try to do too many things at once. But if they show you proudly some fresh fish, order it. They will take good care of it. Red mullet (*barbounia)* and sea bream (*sinagritha)* are good and pricey. *Marithes* (whitebait), baby squid (*kalamarakia)* and octopus (*oktapodhi)* are cheaper. Lobster (*astakos)* is expensive but cheaper than in many countries.

Meat
Since Greece joined the European Community, pork has been gradually ousting lamb as the most-common meat. It is imported and much cheaper, and used extensively now instead of lamb for *souvlakia* (kebab: meat, tomato and onions grilled on a skewer). Meat is grilled or casseroled with vegetables, fish is fried or grilled unless it is very large, when it is baked. Apart from tomato, few sauces are served. A squeeze of lemon replaces them. Dishes are often tastier in islands once occupied by the Italians – and better cooked. Moussaka, favourite dish of most visitors, was really a feast and birthday treat on the Islands, when it was made with lamb and plenty of aubergines. To satisfy tourist demands, they often use beef and potato these days.

Salads and Starters
Greek salads and starters are delicious. *Tzatsiki* (dip of yoghurt, garlic, grated cucumber and olive oil) is best when made with local farm yoghurt (it should be sheep's milk), but even on small

isles some tavernas now use large tins of it imported from Athens. *Taramosalata*, the paste of smoked fish roe, is delicious with bread and wine before the main course. Tomato and cucumber salad (*angour domata)* is improved by a little red and green peppers. Vegetables (usually tomatoes, courgettes or aubergines) stuffed with mince or rice (*yemitses)* are served hot or cold as starters, vegetables or main dish. Vine leaves stuffed with mince or rice (*dolmades)* can be served the same way, or very small ones are served as snacks with drinks.

The great tourist standby is called Greek salad by visitors, village salad by most tavernas, and *horiatiki* by Greeks. Usually it is made of tomato and cucumber wedges, sliced onion and red and green peppers in olive oil, with olives, oregano, salt and pepper, topped with slices of feta (goat cheese) sprinkled with oregano. Cheeses can be goat, sheep or (more rarely) cow. A blue cheese is called *rockfor* (Roquefort!) and a gruyère-style *graviera*. Goat cheese dusted with flour and fried in olive oil or grilled (*saganaki)* can be very good. *Kasseri* is said to be like cheddar but it is usually made from sheep's milk.

Fruit and Puddings
Fruit is delicious (melon, grapes, apricots, apples, wild or cultivated strawberries, according to season and island). Greek yoghurt is excellent. So, though formal restaurants may serve desserts, few island

FOOD AND DRINK

tavernas do (except ice-cream).
You might get cream caramel,
yoghurt with honey and walnuts,
honeycakes (*baklavas*), honey
puffs (*loukoumades*), or
semolina cake with almonds,
cinnamon and lemon (*halvas*).
There are a few formal
restaurants with white table
cloths on smaller islands.
Tavernas are the best place to
eat Greek food. Of these, the
best ask you into the kitchen to
see the fish and meat on the slab
waiting to be cooked and other
dishes bubbling in copper pans
on the stove.
If you order all your meal at
once, it will arrive all together
on cold plates. Try salads with
some wine first, then go to pick
your main dish.
Menus as presented are just a
rough guide. Restaurants and

*The fruit you get on the Greek Isles
is delicious: make the most of it*

tavernas buy what is good and
cheap at the market.

Drink
Cafés (*kafeneions*) serve 'Greek'
coffee, which is Turkish coffee
to us, with mud in the bottom:
sweet is *glyko*, medium is *metrio*,
sugarless is *sketo*. Nescafé is
sometimes called 'American'
coffee, and served iced without
milk or sugar, it is *frappé*.
Ouzo (Greek pastis) is cruder
than French but served the
same way (iced with water).
Retsina (resinated white wine)
originated 3,000 years ago when
Greece was exporting oil and
wine in jars sealed with plaster
and resin. They believed that
resin preserved wine, which it
does not. Either you think it tastes
like camphor balls or paraffin
and hate it, or think it an ideal
accompaniment to Greek food.
The isle of Cephalonia makes the
best dry white wine (Robola) and
also a muscat sweet wine rivalling
the renowned muscat of Samos.
There are reliable brand wines
which you can buy on all except
the smallest isles, such as
Demestica (red and white),
Santa Helena (one of the better
dry whites), and Achaia Clauss
wines. Dry white Hymettus from
near Athens is often available.
Otherwise most islands drink
their own wine and import a
little from an island nearby.
White and red wines are
produced on Kos, Thassos,
Andros, Naxos, Ios, and Milos.
Reds in particular come from
Corfu (try Ropa), Lefkas (very
dark wine called Santa Mavra),
Lemnos (Mavro Kalpaki),
Euboea (Halkidas), Paros (good
deep red, made from Mandilari

grape), Ikaria, Santorini (very strong wines around 17 per cent: Santorini and Vinsanto, much sought by Greeks themselves, and especially sweet Thira, grown on that little isle), and a big producer of powerful red wines, Crete (Malvazia, Mavro Romeika, Peza, Daphnes, Creta). Mavrodaphne, strong sweet red wine, is drunk everywhere. Zakynthos (Zante) has a refreshing dry, white 'green' (young) wine called Verdea. Greek beer is made now by French, Danish and Dutch brewers, is mostly lager, and is expensive compared to wine. For brandy, most Greeks use the name of the big producer Metaxa (3, 5 and 7 star). It is a bit rough for drinking on its own, but is useful for mixed drinks such as brandy sour and Alexander. Drinkable fruit-flavoured spirits are made, some dry as aperitifs, some sweet as liqueurs.

ACCOMMODATION

Accommodation has improved greatly on the Greek Isles but on very small islands there are few hotels or pensions.
In private houses and cheaper pensions showers can be eccentric. Often they have fixed heads forced round to point at the loo and the towel rail, so do not take towels or clothing into the room. A slow central drain in the floor ensures an ankle-deep flood. Water is precious on some small isles. It may go off for part of the day.
Only a few island hotels are specifically recommended in this book (see under individual island), simply because nearly all hotels are fairly small and are

> **Hotel gradings**
> De luxo, A, B, C, D and E. In hotels down to 'B' grade all rooms have private bathrooms; in grade 'C' some have private bathrooms; in grade 'D' and 'E' private facilities seldom exist.

liable to be fully booked. Avoid booking half-board where possible. Eating out at tavernas or café-bars is part of the scene and the best way to meet people. If you want Holiday Inn comfort, stay on Rhodes, Corfu, Crete, Athens or a mainland resort. There are, however, a few big, fairly luxurious hotels on big isles such as Kos and Mykonos.

> **If you arrive without somewhere to stay:**
> ● You will see notices such as 'room rent' on private houses. In mid-summer, especially when the ferry arrives late in the day, do not be too choosy on the first night. At other times see the room first.
> ● If you cannot find a room, ask in a taverna after buying a drink.
> ● Locals often meet ferries, offering rooms. These can be a long walk away and will almost certainly entail sharing the house wc and shower.
> ● Pay a little extra, if possible, for a pension or small hotel. These are likely to be very good value on bigger isles such as Kos, Paros, Zakynthos and Skiathos. On small isles they are more likely to be basic but you may have your own toilet and shower and they are very cheap.

WEATHER/NIGHTLIFE

WEATHER AND WHEN TO GO

Mid-summer (late June, July, August) can be very hot, so take a hat and beach-cover clothes. The meltemi (cool northern wind) provides welcome relief from the heat. The Saronic Isles have their own wind – the north-easterly greggo.

In any other months, take a sweater and trousers for

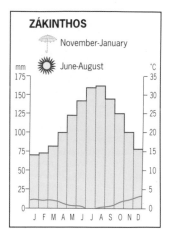

ZÁKINTHOS

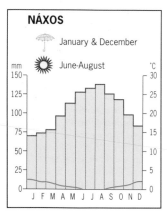

NÁXOS

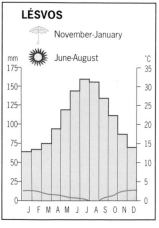

LÉSVOS

evenings. If visiting monasteries, you need a reasonably long skirt, long trousers for men, and something long-sleeved. There is little chance to wear formal clothes on small islands.

If hopping around islands, you must necessarily be something of a back-packer. Do not take more than you can carry comfortably. But do include spare shoes (one sturdy pair), a light sweater and a complete change of clothes. Do not gamble on washing and drying clothes over night – the water may go off. Greek islands are not normally prepared for winter visitors (central heating is very rare). The tourist season is basically April–October.

NIGHTLIFE

Only on big islands or in international hotels is there formal nightlife. But discos of a sort open in cellars, old barns, windmills or bars during the tourist season. You will find one

Like these locals, you may have to wait a long time at a taverna table

on all but the tiniest isles. Bars specialise either in pop music or Greek music. Most Greeks – especially the men – will dance on any excuse. Inpromptu taverna and bar dance evenings are the most fun. Live bouzouki music is played in some tavernas. Bouzoukias are night clubs where the music has become true professional entertainment rather than just Greek exuberance.

Most visitors prefer to have a long meal with wine in or outside a taverna, and see if music and dancing follow.

HOW TO BE A LOCAL

● Never try to hurry a Greek – it is very bad manners. Never appear even to be in a hurry.
● 'Fast food' restaurants are unknown on most isles; be prepared to sit a long time at a taverna table and just enjoy the scene. Eating is a social occasion, and a meal is expected to last all evening.
● Greeks are modest about clothing and will always lean towards more formal dressing, so do not go into a taverna in a bathing costume or stripped to the waist.
● To speak quietly, to be friendly, are signs of good manners. Greeks are polite and helpful and will respond immediately if you are the same. They also love to talk, so if you learn just a few words of Greek you will be an instant success. Never snap your fingers or shout at a waiter or waitress. Never approach a Greek girl without an introduction.
● The siesta is still observed in smaller places. Noise, including driving scooters and motor bikes, is forbidden between 14.00hrs and 17.00hrs; offices and shops are closed, cafés and tavernas open.
● Bargaining is simply not done in hotels, restaurants, big shops, kiosks. It *is* done at street stalls or markets (except for food), so do not be shy.

CHILDREN

The Greeks love children, and like to keep them with them until late in the evening. So you will find no problem in taking children out to eat with you – they will be welcomed in all tavernas and restaurants.

There is little entertainment especially for children in Greece, except in big cities like Athens. But good beaches are mostly what families look for on holiday, and most Greek beaches are safe and ideal for children. The sea is perfect for little ones to swim in.

If your children are not used to the hot sun, do make sure that you take high factor protection cream. Hats are advisable: the mid-summer sun is extremely fierce in Greece.

TIGHT BUDGET

Getting around the Greek Isles on a tight budget is not quite so easy since the clamp-down on sleeping on beaches, but is easier than almost any other country.

● You can walk into a taverna and order simply a salad.

● Rooms in people's houses are very cheap; the facilities may be basic, but will usually be clean.

● Ferry fares are fixed by the Greek Government, but you can often get cheap tourist or even deck class on big ferries from Piraeus (Athens). However, tourist areas can be awash with luggage and uncomfortable in summer heat on long runs. Toilets can be awful.

● If hitch-hiking, look clean.

You may be able to find rooms in private houses, like these picturesque ones on the harbour in Milos

DIRECTORY

Contents

Arriving

(See also individual islands.)

● **Air**: There are scheduled flights to Athens from all over the world and to Kos from many European countries. There are connecting flights from Athens to Atkion (for Lefkas), Cephalonia, Chios, Kos, Lemnos, Leros, Lesbos (Mytilini), Milos, Mykonos, Paros, Samos, Santorini, Skiathos, Skyros, Zante (Zakynthos). Athens airport is divided into two: West (Olympic Airlines domestic and international flights) and East (other international airlines). Allow time for connecting flights. Charter flights (cheaper) are legion from Europe to many islands in high summer, but from the US nearly all charters go to Athens, Rhodes or Crete. Under Greek law, you must be given an accommodation voucher with these cheap flights. Often it is for a campsite or a room in a private house. You do not have to use it, but it must be for actual accommodation.

● **Ferries**: Ferries go to most islands from Piraeus, the port of Athens, although they go also to a few islands from Rafina and Lavrion (both reached by bus from Athens), and Aghios Konstandinos, Kavala, Keramoti, Kimi, Kyllini, Patras, Thessaloniki and Volos (all on the mainland). There are also fast hydrofoil services to some islands from Piraeus, Lavrion, Aghios Konstandinos, Kimi, Thessaloniki and Volos. (For routes, see under individual islands.) There are three basic ways of seeing the islands. You can take a package to a fairly big island and explore it thoroughly, taking an excursion or two to a smaller isle. Or you can pick bed and breakfast, or just a bed, on an isle which has ferries to three or four others, use this as a base to leave most of your luggage, and stay overnight in rooms at any of the other isles if you want or if you cannot get a ferry back. Or you can island hop. This needs as much time as possible, and patience. Ferries to and from some smaller isles are not frequent and can be cancelled because of ill-winds at some times of year. Because of ferry times, you can often see twice as many isles in three weeks as in a fortnight.

Do check ferry sailings and times right up to the day you are going: ferries can be out of action and even switched to another island if it is festival time there! The port police are helpful and give friendly advice on ferry times, but often only speak Greek so you need pencil and paper. For most ferries you must buy your ticket from a local agent – often the grocer's shop – but do not rely on the agent for information. Agents look after rival companies and will not tell you that another boat exists (especially true in Piraeus). Asking in a taverna can be more reliable. Tickets can sometimes be purchased on the quayside or aboard the ferries.

More ferries run from about mid-May to early September and in June, July and August there may be many excursions to other islands. One trick is to take an excursion and jump ship, but do tell the boat crew.

Above all, leave time to get the aircraft home. If you miss a charter flight, you cannot transfer to another, and a scheduled flight will cost you dear.

• **Visas**: No visas are needed by Britons, other EC members, US citizens, Canadians, Australians or New Zealanders for stays up to three months. No foreigner is supposed to work in Greece without a work permit. Penalties for illegal working are severe.

Baby Equipment
Do not count on small island pharmacies or grocers stocking your particular brand of baby-milk or food. It is safest to bring your own. Disposable nappies (diapers) are available, except on very small isles.

Camping
Camping outside official sites has been illegal since 1977. Officially this was because hordes of young people camped on or alongside beaches and caused sanitation and fire hazards. An unstated reason was an official policy to upgrade tourism and to discourage hippies or young people with no money to spend. The authorities believed that youngsters without money would turn to crime in order to eat, and that hanging around beaches, bars and cafés discouraged other visitors. 'Private' campsites are usually cheap, unofficial, and have minimal facilities. Official sites, with fairly good facilities, are dearer. Obtaining gas cylinders for cookers can be difficult in some areas. *Never* light an open fire: you will probably get 2–3 months in prison.

Until recently, it was possible, though illegal, to sleep on beaches in a sleeping bag. The police have clamped down on this and you could easily end up in jail, not a good idea in Greece.

Crime
Greek islanders are mainly extremely honest. Virtually all robberies, petty thefts from pockets, rooms or cars are done by foreign visitors who run out of money. See **Police**, page 121.
Drugs: In no circumstances take

illegal drugs into Greece – you will do a long stretch in a primitive prison. If you take medical drugs, take a doctor's certificate with them.

Domestic Travel

Hiring self-drive transport can be a problem on isles with rough roads. Only hire a motor-bike if you are an accomplished and steady rider. Mopeds can be very dangerous and some package-tour operators actively discourage moped hire. Servicing is slack, so make absolutely sure that brakes and steering are good. Italian mopeds are giving way to automatic Japanese models. Up steep hills or up fairly reasonable hills with two aboard, they may stop or jump out of gear.

It is vital to have good medical insurance for Greece. Before hiring a vehicle, make certain that you are covered for road accidents. Many policies are void for mopeds.

● **Car Hire** Now that Greece is in the EC, valid British driving licences are accepted. Americans will probably need an International Driving Licence.

Car hire is expensive, with tax and mileage added, but it is the best way of seeing most islands, especially real old farming villages. Rewards are great. You need care and some courage to drive dirt mule tracks which pass for roads. You *must* have a collision waiver, otherwise you can be charged outrageously for a scratch and pay up to £500 of repair bills whether the damage was your fault or not. Be careful of cut-price local hire

Hydriot children in national costume on one of the island's festival days

firms. Their servicing is often appalling, they may refuse the accident waive clause and take little interest if you break down. Check brakes, tyres, including spare, before hiring. If possible, hire from Avis, Eurocar or Hertz, even if it costs more. Fill up with petrol when you can – garages are scarce in country districts.

● **Speed limits** Private vehicles: Built-up areas 31mph (50kph); outside built-up areas 43mph (70kph); motorways 62mph (100kph). You must carry fire extinguishers, first aid kit, breakdown warning triangle. Undipped headlights must not be used in towns.

● **Maps** Some local island maps are a joke. Uncompleted or planned-but-not-started roads may be marked. Hard-earth mule tracks are marked as roads because local people use them. Do not shy away from them or you will miss a lot, but watch for transmission-shattering

DIRECTORY

Idyllic peace and quiet on the waterfront, Zakynthos

projecting boulders. Michelin map 980 of Greece is very useful but does not show these minor roads which you will need to explore properly. Do not worry if you get lost. There are not enough roads for you to be lost for long.

● **Car Breakdown** Motoring organisations are not represented on most Greek isles. Where help is available, dial 104.

● **Buses** These vary greatly from isle to isle in frequency and routes. Timetables are usually posted outside tavernas or cafés by main stops, but are somewhat unreliable. Buses can be early or very late. Mid-summer they are very crowded and you may have to stand on one foot and fight to get on or off at intermediate stops. There is no orderly queuing to get on but you will not be left behind if it is humanly possible to squeeze you on – all part of Island life.

● **Taxis** In high-summer it pays to share taxis, which cost more but have great advantages. To tour an island in a day, find three or four people to share a taxi with you, agree the cost before you set out and try to pick an English-speaking driver who can tell you about the passing scene.

Electricity

Generally 220 volts, though 110 on some remote isles. Two-pronged plugs are common – take a plug adaptor for shavers, irons, hairdryers etc.

Embassies and Consulates

Great Britain – 1 Ploutarchou Street, Athens 106 75 (tel: (01) 7236211-19). 24 Akti Possidonis, Piraeus (tel: (01) 4178345).
USA–91 Vasilissis Sofias Avenue, Athens 115 21 (tel: (01) 7212951/9).
Canada–4 Ioannou Gennadiou Street, Athens 115 21 (tel: (01) 7239511/9).
Australia–37 D. Soutsou Street, Athens 115 21 (tel: (01) 6447303).
New Zealand–15-17 An. Tsochou Street, Athens 115 21 (tel: (01) 6410311/5).

Emergency numbers
See **Police** for each island.

Entertainment information
On posters or ask in tavernas.

Hazards
Mosquitoes are a curse in Greece. Take the usual precaution of not opening a window with the light on. But do take an electric mosquito killer with an adaptor plug. They are a superb invention. Coils stink. Some lotions are effective, too: try Jaico anti-Mosquito Milk.

Health
Under EC agreements, European visitors can receive free medical treatment. You must have a current E111 form before leaving home. But do take out extra medical insurance. For serious illness it is essential. Some package tours offer medical insurance at extra charge. Make sure that the policy covers motor accidents and the cost of an air taxi (needed on some isles to take you to a bigger island, or to Athens). Better still, have a policy which will fly you home in an emergency. Many Greek hospitals are poorly equipped and staffed.
Private doctors are expensive. You will have to pay and claim on your insurance when you return. There should be at least one doctor (*iatro*) on each island (hours usually 09.00–13.00hrs; 17.00–19.00hrs). Hospitals occur less frequently. Outpatients clinics are held in the mornings. The Tourist Police on each island will be able to supply addresses and phone numbers.

Health Regulations
No special immunisation needed, but check that your shots are up to date – smallpox vaccination, typhoid, tetanus.

Holidays
Each island has a holiday on its Saint's Day and on annual festival days. For the following national holidays *all* shops and businesses shut (except perhaps the baker's shop), and also close on the afternoon before and the morning after. If a holiday falls on Sunday, Monday is also a holiday. Orthodox Easter – a great two-day festival of religious services and processions. The date varies.
1 January – New Year's Day.
6 January – Epiphany.
25 March – Greek Independence Day.
Shrove Monday.
Good Friday.
Easter Sunday.
Easter Monday.
1 May – May Day (Labour Day).
7 June – Day of the Holy Spirit.
15 August – Assumption of the Virgin Mary.
28 October – Ochi Day (anniversary of Metaxas saying *Ochi* (No) to Mussolini's demands in World War II).
25 December – Christmas.
26 December – St Stephen's Day (Boxing Day).

Lost Property
Go to the police if only for insurance purposes, but unless the property is very valuable, they take little interest.

Money Matters
Credit cards are not used on the Islands except in higher grade hotels and restaurants and more expensive shops in the bigger

DIRECTORY

towns. Travellers' cheques are sometimes suspect outside these establishments or banks (*trapeza*). Normal banking hours are 08.00hrs to 13.30/14.00hrs (usually closed Saturdays and Sundays). The main banks are the National Bank of Greece and the Commercial Bank of Greece. Most small islands have no bank. Usually there is an exchange office in a travel agent or grocer's shop, but watch exchange rates here, and in big hotels. Foreign currency is always in demand, especially dollars, pounds sterling and deutschmarks. British bank cheques are cashed in banks displaying the EC (Eurocheque) sign, but you must present a Eurocheque card. Home bank cards are not accepted outside Britain or the US. You may take 100,000 drachmas into Greece in local currency, but may export only 20,000 in denominations of 1,000.

Nudism
Nudism is still banned on all but a very few nudist beaches. There are on some islands remote beaches where nudism is tolerated; for example, at Krassa, now called Banana Beach because you can peal off everything, on Skiathos. Topless sunbathing has become more general, and is tolerated except in the centre of town. On Kos, for instance, it is usual alongside the harbour bay in Kos Town.

Opening Times
Banks: 08.00–13.30/14.00hrs Monday to Friday, some open Saturdays in big towns.
Museums:closed on Mondays or Tuesdays; normally other weekdays 08.30hrs–15.00hrs, outdoor sites to 19.00hrs. Winter hours are usually shorter.
Post Offices: 07.00–15.00hrs, Monday to Friday.
Shops: open in summer 08.30–13.30 and 17.30–20.30hrs on Tuesday, Thursday and Friday; 08.30–14.00hrs on Monday, Wednesday and Saturday. But in tourist areas in summer they usually open Monday to Saturday 08.00– 13.00hrs, then 17.00 until 20.30–22.00hrs. Souvenir and tourist shops open on Sundays.

Pharmacies
For minor complaints, Greeks consult pharmacists (*farmakio*), who are able to dispense directly some drugs and medicines only available on prescription in other countries.

Photography
The light and colours make Greece a magnificent country for amateur photographers. The light in summer is usually stronger than it seems and can ruin pictures. Museums charge a fee for taking pictures (no charge at archaeological sites). Varieties of films (instamatic or 35mm) are sold on many islands, but are more expensive than at home. Do not take pictures on airfields (most of which are both civil and military) or of radar installations. Plane spotters are totally misunderstood, too.

Place names
You will find words in Roman script spelt several different ways. Twice the Greek Government has issued official spellings but almost no-one has taken much notice. There are also alternative spellings and

names to many islands. Notable are Zante (officially Zakynthos), and Lesbos (officially Mytilini). The official name is in timetables. For islands and places we have tried to follow those names and spellings used by British and American tour operators and airlines, but these vary, too. You may well find it useful to learn at least the letters of the Greek alphabet, so that you can recognise place names on maps.

Police

Greek Tourist Police (usually in an office in the police station) are helpful. You can tell them from other policemen by a flag on their pockets showing which languages they speak.

Alas, they are growing scarcer. The harshness or flexibility with which the Greek police apply the law can vary from island to island. You *can* be arrested for nude bathing or sunbathing. You *will* be arrested for getting involved in a brawl, drunken fight or for offensive behaviour. If you carry drugs you will be in *real* trouble. You could get life imprisonment for passing round a 'joint'. You will get 1–3 years at least for possessing even a small amount of cannabis, and Greek jails, they say, are not to be recommended.

Post

Signs of post offices (*tachidromio*) and post boxes are conveniently painted bright yellow. In small places, mail is not delivered to houses, but to a village centre – bakery, café, shop. Stamps can be bought at Post Offices or kiosks –*periptera* (small tax). Overseas mail can be sent surface or airmail.

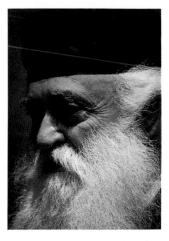

The face of a monk from St John the Divine Monastery on Patmos

Telephone and telegraph offices and separate from post offices.

Religion

Greeks mostly belong to the Eastern Orthodox Church; there are some Catholics, especially on isles that were formerly Italian. Even those who are not seemingly religious regard the church with great respect. During the Turkish occupation, it was the symbol and rallying point for Greek culture, language and for freedom.

Siesta

Legally, all noise, including riding motorbikes and scooters, is prohibited between 14.00hrs and 17.00hrs in towns and villages, and after 23.00hrs in built-up areas. The afternoon can be a good time for looking around, but the heat can be fierce so *do* take a sun hat. Tavernas and cafés mostly stay open.

DIRECTORY

Student and Youth Travel

The best card to have is the International Student Identity Card (ISIC). If you are under 22 it can get you discounts on museums entrance, theatre tickets, archaeological sites and some local travel. If under 26, cheap air fares may be found through STA Travel (tel: 071 937 9921), or USIT/Campus Travel (tel: 071 730 3402).

Telephones

You can telephone or send telegrams from 'OTE' offices. Opening hours vary greatly. Overseas dialling codes are: Australia 00 61; Canada and USA 00 1; Ireland 00 353; UK 00 44 New Zealand 00 64; (then minus the initial '0' of the area code). Inland Service numbers: Directory Enquiries 131; Police 100; Medical Emergency 166; Fire 199; Roadside assistance 104; Telegrams-cables 165.

Time

Greek time is Eastern European, 2 hours ahead of Greenwich Mean Time.

Tipping

Not so widespread as in some countries. In high-class restaurants it is 10 per cent, but in tavernas or little restaurants small loose change suffices.

Toilets

Not the Greeks' strong point, even in little pensions. Public toilets are rare on the islands. It is best to order a drink or coffee in a taverna and use their toilet. Even that is liable to be primitive.

Tourist Offices

Greek National Offices:
Great Britain – 4 Conduit Street, London W1R 0DJ (tel: 071-734 5997).

USA – Olympic Tower, 645 Fifth Avenue, 5th Floor, New York , NY 10022 (tel: 212-421 5777). Nat. Bank of Greece Building, Suite 600, 168 N. Michigan Avenue, Chicago, Illonois 60601 (tel: 312-782 1084). 611 West Sixth Street, Suite 2198, Los Angeles, California 90017 (tel: 213-626 6696).

Australia and New Zealand – 51-57 Pitt Street, Sydney, NSW 2000 (tel: 02-2411 663/4).

Canada – 1300 Bay Street, Main Level, Toronto, Ontario (tel: 416-968 2220). 1233 rue de la Montagne, Suite 101, Montreal, Quebec (tel: 514-871 1535).

Greece:
Athens – 2 Amerikis Street, Athens 10564 (tel: (01) 3223111).
Port of Piraeus – Directorate of Tourism of East Mainland Greece and the Islands, Marina Zeas, 18504 (tel: (01) 4135716). ·
On islands – Big islands with EOT offices include:-
Kos—Akti Koundouriotou Street, Kos Town (tel: (0242) 28724). Cephalonia—Argostoli (tel: (0671) 22248/24466).
For other islands, see text for **Tourist Office** and **Tourist Police** telephone numbers.

Travel Agencies

On larger isles there are private travel agencies, usually in fierce competition. Useful for booking ferry and air tickets but they will not help you with ferry companies they do not represent. Be especially wary in Piraeus as they will tell you that there is no ferry to an island on a certain day as it is run by a company they do *not* represent.

LANGUAGE

Unless you know the Greek script, a vocabulary is not of very much use to the visitor. But it is helpful to know the alphabet, so that you can find your way around; and the following few basic words and phrases will help too. (See also **Food and Drink** chapter, page 108).

Alphabet

Alpha	Αα	short a, as in hat
Beta	Ββ	v sound
Gamma	Γγ	guttural g sound
Delta	Δδ	hard th, as in father
Epsilon	Εε	short e
Zita	Ζζ	z sound
Eta	Ηη	long e, as in feet
Theta	Θθ	soft th, as in think
Iota	Ιι	short i, as in hit
Kappa	Κκ	k sound
Lambda	Λλ	l sound
Mu	Μμ	m sound

As in all holiday destinations, tourist and souvenir shops abound; this one is on Mykonos

Nu	Νν	n sound
Xi	Ξξ	x or ks sound
Omicron	Οο	short o, as in pot
Pi	Ππ	p sound
Rho	Ρρ	r sound
Sigma	Σσ	s sound
Taf	Ττ	t sound
Ipsilon	Υυ	another ee sound, or y as in funny
Phi	φφ	f sound
Chi	Χχ	guttural ch, as in loch
Psi	Ψψ	ps, as in chops
Omega	Ωω	long o, as in bone

Numbers

1	éna	14	dekatéssera
2	dío	15	dekapénde
3	tria	16	dekaéxi
4	téssera	17	dekaeptá
5	pénde	18	dekaokto
6	éxi	19	dekaennía
7	eptá	20	ikosi
8	októ	30	triánda
9	ennía	40	saránda
10	déka	50	peнínda
11	éndeka	100	ekató
12	dódeka	101	ekaton éna
13	dekatría	1000	chília

LANGUAGE

Basic vocabulary

good morning	kaliméra
good evening	kalispéra
goodnight	kaliníkta
goodbye	chérete
hello	yásou
thank you	efcharistó
please/you are welcome	parakaló
yes	ne
no	óchi
where is ...?	poo íne?
how much is ...?	póso káni?
I would like	tha íthela
do you speak English?	milate angliká?
I don't speak Greek	then miló helliniká

Places

street	ódos
avenue	léofóros
square	platía
restaurant	estiatório
hotel	xenodochío
room	domátio
post office	tachithromío
letter	grámma
stamps	grámmatóssima
police	astinomía
customs	teloniakos
passport	diavatirion
pharmacy	farmakío
doctor	iatrós
dentist	odontiatros
entrance	ísothos
exit	éxothos
bank	trápeza
church	eklisía
hospital	nosokomío
café	kafeneion

Travelling

car	aftokínito
bus	leoforio
train	tréno
boat	karávi
train station	stathmos
bus station	stasi ton leoforio

airport	aerodromio
ticket	isitirio

Food

food	fagitó
bread	psomi
water	neró
wine	krasí
beer	bira
coffee	kafé

Fish

lobster	astakós
squid	kalamarákia
octopus	oktapóthi
red mullet	barboúnia
whitebait	maríthes
sea bream	sinagritha

Meat/poultry

lamb	arnáki
chicken	kotópoulo
meat balls	kefthedes
meat on a skewer	souvlákia
liver	skóti

Vegetables

spinach	spanáki
courgette	kolokithia
beans	fasolia

Salads and Starters

olives	eliés
yoghurt and cucumber dip	tzatsiki
tomato and cucumber salad	angour domata
stuffed vine leaves	dolmades
'Greek' salad with cheese	horiatiki

Desserts

honeycake	baklavá
honey puffs	loukoumádes
semolina cake	halvá
ice cream	pagotó
yoghurt	yiaourti
custard tart	bougatsa

Page numbers in *italics* refer to illustrations

INDEX

ACKNOWLEDGEMENTS

The Automobile Association would like to thank the following photographers and libraries for their assistance in the compilation of this book

J ALLAN CASH PHOTOLIBRARY 23 Tinos Town, 30 Pottery, Siphnos, 35 Church at Plaka, 52 Akrotiri, 58/9 White Rocks Hotel, 62 Assos Bay, 65 Fruit Market, 67 Vrontis Bay, 113 Men at Tavern, 121 Monk, 123 Gift Shop. INTERNATIONAL PHOTOBANK 11 Temple at Aphaia, 13 Aegina, 77 Kalymnos. NATURE PHOTOGRAPHERS LTD 97 Gull (T Ennis), 98 Hawkmoth, 101 Wheatear (K Carlson), 99 Whip Snake, 105 Bee Orchid (P Sterry), 102 Fir Tree, 104 Turtle (J Sutherland).

SPECTRUM COLOUR LIBRARY Cover Thira, 15 Poros, 17 Hydra, 18 Fishermen, 20 Spetses, 25 Mykonos, 29 Church at Siphnos, 41 Lunch, 43 Antiparos, 45 Naxos Town, 47 Ios, 50/1 Kamari Beach, 53 Vineyards, 55 Shoe Repairer, 56 Defini Bay, 61 Sami, 70/1 Olympos, 72 Symi, 79 Patmos, 82 Pythagorion, 87 Mending Nets, 94 Rigo Beach, 96 Skopelos, 107 Worry Beads, 108 Patmos, 110 Melons. ZEFA PICTURE LIBRARY (UK) LTD 4 Skopelos Harbour, 8 Skiathos, 9 Thira, 10 Skopelos, 26 Windmill, 32 Seriphos, 37 Livadi Harbour, 49 Santorini, 75 Kas, 84 Chios, 88/9 Lisbos, 90 Lemnos, 114 Milos, 117 Hydra, 118 Zakynthos.